ACRL PUBLICATIONS IN LIBRARIANSHIP NO. 61

FRAMING LIBRARY INSTRUCTION

by John Budd

Association of College and Research Libraries
A division of the American Library Association
Chicago, 2009

The paper used in this publication meets the minimum requirements of American National Standard for Information Sciences-Permanence of Paper for Printed Library Materials, ANSI Z39.48-1992. ∞

Library of Congress Cataloging-in-Publication Data

Budd, John, 1953-
 Framing library instruction / by John Budd.
    p. cm. -- (ACRL publications in librarianship ; no. 61)
 Includes bibliographical references and index.
  ISBN 978-0-8389-8513-7 (pbk. : alk. paper) 1. Information literacy--Study and teaching (Higher) 2. Information resources--Evaluation--Study and teaching (Higher) 3. Critical thinking--Study and teaching (Higher) 4. Library orientation for college students. 5. Academic libraries--Relations with faculty and curriculum. I. Title.
  ZA3075.B83 2009
  028.7071'1--dc22
                              2009038344

Printed in the United States of America.

13 12 11 10 09   5 4 3 2 1

TABLE OF CONTENTS

Acknowledgements

I owe a debt to a number of people who have contributed to my thinking about instruction, especially to the course that is outlined in Chapter Six. My thanks go out to Goodie Bhullar, Rachel Brekhus, Diane Hunter, Chris LeBeau, Karen Robinson, Frances Piesbergen, Carrie Donovan, Cate McGowan, Noël Kopriva, and Kira Green. I would also like to thank Craig Gibson, editor of the Publications in Librarianship monograph series, and the editorial board members who offered invaluable comments and suggestions; they have made the book better.

CHAPTER ONE

A Framework for Instruction

An undergraduate student today is flooded by "stuff." Some of the stuff has to do with life and living (frequently related to being on one's own for the first time). Some of it has to do with being introduced to new topics of study (courses on topics they have not studied before). Some of the stuff includes the vast world of information, especially the information that a library can provide access to. The predicament students face is one reason Christine Bruce, a faculty member at Queensland University of Technology in Australia, says, "Information literacy is conceivably the foundation for learning in our contemporary environment of continuous technological change" (Christine Susan Bruce, "Information Literacy as a Catalyst for Educational Change: A Background Paper," http://eprints.qut.edu.au/archive/00004977/01/4977.pdf). Even given the predicament of information overload, this is a very strong claim; throughout this book it will be revisited—as an epistemological statement, as a manifesto, and as a pedagogical goal. The literature on information literacy and the instruction libraries provide in general is large, so a reader (or potential reader) may wonder if another work is needed. This book is actually an extended argument for taking a new look at instruction. The Association of College and Research Libraries (ACRL), in the form of Standards, attempts to provide a foundation for instruction and, specifically, for information literacy. When an association deems an issue of sufficient importance that standards are written, those standards must be taken seriously. A part of the argument here, though, is to question that foundation. The questioning is respectful of the aims of the Standards and the enormous amount of thought and consideration that went into composing them. But the primary intention of this book is twofold: to construct a different foundation for instruction, and to build a pragmatic program upon that foundation. Toward these ends, the book will challenge some stated ideas about instruction and suggest a fairly specific application of the alternative foundation.

A beginning point for an investigation into instruction programs in libraries is inquiring into learning and thinking. The starting point arises from a presumed purpose of such programs: to enable students to succeed academically, to learn effectively, and to grow intellectually (see, for example, the goals stated by the Lafayette College Library, http://library.lafayette.edu/instruction/infolit_define). *Note: this presumed purpose does not include use of the library, ability to search catalogs or databases, or other competencies.* They are absent, not because they are unimportant, but because they are means to ends. In other words, the instruction programs do not exist for libraries or librarians and are not about tools (print, electronic, etc.).

The purpose does not have its basis in the endeavor itself, but in the potential the endeavor presents to others. The engineer does have to know about materials, instrumentation, and many other things, but the engineer also (and primarily) has to think about how people might use what they design, how the fruits of their labor will affect people. Most people have used systems (technical and human) that have apparently been constructed for those within the system. Use of it may be problematic because of obscure language, opaque procedures, or dead ends. Such systems fail because they do not achieve the primary goal of enabling people to accomplish what they want. So, the teacher must think about what and how students learn and what the students can do with what they learn.

While the intention here is not to review the vast literature on instructional programs, a few notable works should be mentioned at the outset. These works are mentioned here because they also mark processes of questioning foundations and putting instruction into action. One is a book by James Elmborg and Sheril Hook, *Centers for Learning: Libraries and Writing Centers in Collaboration* (2005). They explore the connection between the writing process (and the thinking that goes along with it) and the quest to become informed. Jack Andersen (2006) discusses information literacy in the context of sociopolitical discourse. The student's or other information seeker's action is similar to the activities of reading and writing; all of the actions are mediated by society and its communication mechanisms. Heidi Julien and Lisa Given (2002/03) examine the separation that can exist between faculty and academic librarians. In part the gap is perceptual (in that some faculty members may see a bigger difference than is actually present); in part the gap is experiential (in that the two groups approach the goal of student learning via distinct pathways). The day-to-day activities of faculty and librarians are sufficiently different that some communication challenges can manifest themselves. In their extensive investigation Esther Grassian and Joan Kaplowitz (2001) begin with an observation that should never be far from instructors' minds: "People learn when it is meaningful for them to do so" (p. 10). The importance of their observation cannot be overstated, and it informs what is to follow here. There is also a wealth of work outside our field that we can draw on in the development and offering of programs. For example, Barbara Hofer (2004) emphasizes what she refers to as the regulative aspects of knowing (including volition, motivation, and other factors) that are necessary to an examination of an individual's state of awareness, especially of the need to know more than she or he does.

These contributions to thought in programs are valuable; they rightly emphasize the vital element of students' participating in learning and building knowledge. Work in the area of pedagogy today takes student action as a given, an incontrovertible necessity. This is not to say that conveying information is not needed at times, but students are more likely to learn if they have been active in the process. This idea is not new; early in the seventeenth century René Descartes (1989 [1737]) wrote that he is more likely to retain what he learned if he participated first-hand in discovery (p. 21). It may not be an overstatement to say that Descartes pioneered problem-based learning. Attention to student engagement has finally and rightly surpassed concentration on lecture and recitation as the most viable teaching method, at least in the literature of education. Moving forward, we are now faced with the challenge of figuring out what kind of engagement, and to what end, is the most effective in instructional programs. In this book I suggest that a particular framework holds the most promise for us—phenomenological cognitive action. I am using technical language here for a reason. The terminology draws from other fields where definitions are established; this usage is intended to make the explicit connection with the other fields, and also to communicate directly with the people in those fields. Librarianship borrows terminology frequently; this is one more instance. The "action" element is the most self-evident; students make decisions and then act on the basis of the decisions. But how do they decide; what do they consider in pondering possibilities? How do they evaluate alternatives? How do they recognize when they do not know something, but would like to know? How do they ask questions?

Many more questions could accompany these, and more questions will arise throughout this book. As we will see, "action" is a rich concept that carries numerous denotations and connotations. To add to the complexity, "cognition" and "phenomenology" are even richer in their implications. Since college students (of the traditional ages) are still developing cognitively, all efforts in instruction should have an objective aimed at training their minds to assimilate, synthesize, and draw conclusions. In the informational world the assessment of what is presented is almost universally recognized as vital. Libraries' instruction programs are well positioned to enhance this critical ability in students, so the "cognitive" element of the framework is essential. The "phenomenological" element is the most complex, but it draws from a philosophical tradition that fits well with what libraries do. Phenomenology is characterized by the first-person examination of experience, as experience is shaped by intentionality, conceptions of self and other, and the search for truth. One aspect of phenomenology—intentionality—refers to students' doing what they do for particular reasons *and* the reasons themselves can and should be subject to scrutiny. For example, academic success can be examined closely so as to capture everything that success can mean. Another aspect of phenomenology is the recognition of other people as other selves, others who have their own intentionality that may include knowledge, motives, and biases. What is presented by others, then, is not merely objective statements from a disembodied source; it is a human creation and should be read as such. In summary, this framework consists of:

- Phenomenology—the intersubjective relationship of students' intentional search for understanding through the statements, images, or voices of others, and the teachers' engagement of students in those searches
- Cognition—students' ways of thinking about the academic (primarily) challenges they face (through their assignments, papers they write, and explorations they undertake in all of their course work), and also the introduction of metacognitive processes that can help them respond to the challenges

- Action—the students' direct interaction with complex discourse (what others write, say, and show), and the resources that can help them locate the discourse

The framework presents a challenge to librarianship, but one that can be met.

One thing must be made clear at this time. Librarians have a wealth of knowledge, extending to the structure of information conveyors, the organization of ideas, the evaluation of content, and communication with information seekers (among other things). This expertise is a necessary component for instruction programs in libraries. It is not, however, sufficient. The additional piece of the puzzle has to do with teaching—educating. Clarity of presentation is one part of the teaching, but the appropriateness of what is said for the students is even more important. By appropriateness I mean pertinence to what students are learning in their educational programs in general, understandable to students in their cognitive states, and of assistance to students as they try to comprehend the learning process itself. One tactic that many teachers employ is to locate the present state of awareness and knowledge of students in a class. The tactic is intended to provide a reference point that can guide the teacher. Examples, situations, metaphors, etc. flow from that reference point. It helps provide grounding for understanding so that misunderstanding may be minimized.

The questions asked above, along with necessary attention to accreditation, demand that librarians pay attention to the Standards set out by ACRL. The ACRL Standards (2000) will be considered at length in the next chapter, but they do, as has been noted, establish a kind of foundation for instruction as it is practiced today. This context is most clearly stated in the definition of information literacy that prefaces the standards themselves:

> Because of the escalating complexity of [the technological] environment, individuals are faced with diverse, abundant information choices—in their academic studies, in the workplace, and in their personal lives. Information is available through libraries, community resources, special interest organizations, media, and the Internet—and increasingly, information comes to individuals in unfiltered formats, raising questions

> about its authenticity, validity, and reliability. In addition, information is available through multiple media, including graphical, aural, and textual, and these pose new challenges for individuals in evaluating and understanding it. The uncertain quality and expanding quantity of information pose large challenges for society. The sheer abundance of information will not in itself create a more informed citizenry without a complementary cluster of abilities necessary to use information effectively (p. 2).

The lengthy passage is included here because of what we can call the communicative action of the definition. First, it would be impossible to take issue with what is said; every element of the definition is accurate. The media, the abundance, the questions of quality are all genuine and immediate concerns. Further, every aspect has serious implications for education, but they can lead to an overemphasis on mechanics. What is missing is an overarching goal centered on learning, thinking, and critically apprehending what is read, seen, and heard. If these are indeed desiderata, libraries' instructional programs need to address them.

Students and Cognition

Any course or entire instructional program has to begin with instructors' understanding of the cognitive states of students. In one of the most astute introductions to the topic of consciousness, Colin McGinn (1999) warns that the ideas of causation that are learned in connection with the natural sciences and the physical phenomena they deal with are less than adequate to explain human action. He adds, "The fact is that we have no good theory about the nature of mental causation, no model for how reasoning leads to choice. So we try to conceive this in terms we are familiar with, thus distorting the phenomenon. Mental causation is mysterious, which is not a bit surprising given that consciousness and the self are also mysterious" (p. 167). His advocacy of mysteriousness is not shared by all philosophers of the mind, though. Perhaps the most prominent contrarian is Daniel Dennett. According to him, mental causation is not mysterious; it is a purely physical and material function. A metaphor he is fond of using is the "multiple drafts model." The multiple drafts metaphor, for Dennett, is intended to replace the "Cartesian Theater" metaphor. The latter concept refers to a place in the brain where sensory perceptions converge and are ordered so that the perceiver (the person who owns the brain) can become conscious of the perceptions. The Cartesian theater is erroneous, says Dennett (1991), because, "all varieties of perception—indeed, all varieties of thought or mental activity—are accomplished in the brain by parallel, multitrack processes of interpretation and elaboration or sensory inputs. Information entering the nervous system is under continuous 'editorial revision'" (p. 111).

It appears that McGinn and Dennett could never reach agreement on what constitutes consciousness and how cognition works. For the purposes of examining students' apprehension and integration of the thought of others, their differences do matter. The differences will be explored in a later chapter. That said, they both provide extremely useful guidance in our comprehension of how minds (or brains if you prefer) operate. There are a number of additional useful concepts offered by philosophers and cognitive scientists that can be appropriated for instructional programs. Another is the idea of intentionality (mentioned above), as described by John Searle (2002): "'Intentionality' is the name that philosophers and psychologists give to that feature of many of our mental states by which they are directed at, or about states of affairs in the world" (p. 12). Intentionality, defined this way, sounds straightforward (it is each individual's experiencing of the world). The value of the concept may be particularly recognized as a reminder to all teachers that the subject matter of a class offered by the library is not really an end *in and for itself.* The subject matter fits with that of other courses and experiences as some means that students can employ to engage in action. That is, what students learn has a very special kind of utility—the students can build upon what they learn so that they can live their lives. Searle (2002) again provides insightful description of the purpose: "The intrinsic intentionality of the agent is doing all the work. To see this point notice that the psychological explanation of my doing long division is not the algorithm, but my *mastery* of the algorithm and my *intentionally* going through the steps of the algorithm" [emphasis in original] (p. 123).

In more specific terms, instructors should be aware of some of the challenges that are inherent in education. Perhaps the most persistent error that many teachers fall prey to is one of presumption. Teachers tend to presume that somehow, somewhere, at some previous time, students have acquired experiences and intellectual development. Given the presumption, a course can begin in the middle, as it were. The syllabus eschews background that, teachers believe, students should already be aware of. For example, instructors in libraries' programs may presume that, since students have used textbooks for years, the students comprehend indexing principles that are integral to the structure of those textbooks. Suppose that, throughout elementary and secondary schooling, no teacher had ever explained the thinking about categories that underlies indexing and the uses to which it could be put. No doubt many students will have worked out the nature of indexing for themselves, but not all will have done so. McGinn's explanation is more basic still, but it is powerfully instructive: "Our concepts of consciousness are fixed by our own introspective abilities, which is why we cannot form the concept of a bat's consciousness; in addition, we cannot grasp a theory that requires us to transcend our own introspectively based concepts. Suppose you had never seen the color red, but to understand a certain theory you would need to possess the concept *red*: then you simply grasp that theory, period" (1999, pp. 53-54).

Instructional programs have been a mainstay in academic libraries for several decades now. Librarians have been thinking and writing about the programs all this time. If there is any frustration felt by librarians because this instruction has not been perfected, we should all remember that education in general is not perfect, and educational systems have been around for a very long time. Some issues persist, though, even with more consideration and more application. One matter that has been considered for years is whether the instruction should stand alone or be integrated into the general curriculum. Evan Ira Farber (2007) has been a pioneer and a persistent advocate for librarian-faculty collaboration. The program he instituted at Earlham College continues to influence thought and practice at other institutions. In the tradition of Farber, Hannelore Rader (1999) has observed (rightly) that collaboration has tended to succeed where there is careful planning, understanding that faculty guide the primary learning activities on campus, and there is continuous and iterative evaluation. As is the case with most issues in the world of education, there are intellectual/conceptual aspects and there are practical aspects.

On the conceptual side, integration has many merits related to cognition. A cohesive programmatic effort aimed at students' learning the thought and writings on a subject in conjunction with learning the subject matter itself has the potential to enable students to gain knowledge through multiple, sometimes dialectical, ways. This observation deserves a bit of development. In many, if not most, freshman- and sophomore-level courses the readings are prescribed. If students are to delve into the thought of others, they do so at least as much to fulfill the details of assignments as to learn. This sounds like a damning accusation, but it constitutes a stage in learning. In order to advance, the students have to master some procedural steps relating to, for example, the refinement of expression of their thoughts. Even within a single course (and certainly among the courses a student takes) there are tensions and contradictions that manifest themselves in the readings selected for the course. One writer may present a particular view or interpretation of, say, the construction of the U.S. Constitution. Another writer may suggest a quite different view. Effectiveness of learning necessitates that students examine, with the help of the teacher, the logic and reasoning—as well as the ideology (not used here in a pejorative sense)—of the divergent arguments. Dialectical investigation can go farther than individual arguments, encompassing frameworks or programs in an effort to resolve the contradictions.

Engaging in dialectic (n the Hegelian sense of examination of thesis and antithesis as a way to reach a synthesis) is possible for an individual, but it is likely to be better understood in group situations, such as classes. Something akin to Socratic dialogues could involve students in thinking through contradictions and anomalies. Dialectical engagement, at least in some fields of study, can result in more authentic learning than the transmission of information (students being told things). Here is where the conceptual merits of the integrated approach may be most clearly manifested. As students examine opposing thoughts within the context of specific subject matter, the structure of information resources can be introduced. In a later chapter, when course design is discussed in greater detail, specific examples of the distinctions (i.e., theoretical, practical, political) among resources will be offered. There is no doubt that dialectical examination is difficult; there can be resistance on the parts of both students and teachers. Dialectic entails tension, and people may avoid tension-causing situations. For the approach to succeed, teachers will be required to understand dialectics themselves, perhaps with the inclusion of engaging in it themselves. Librarians involved in the instruction should also have such an understanding. [Apart from the instructional programs, librarianship would benefit from a dialectical approach to the most pressing issues.]

Although it usually is not spoken of as such, dialectic is a key teaching and learning approach. Versions were used by Plato and Aristotle, primarily to introduce questioning and answering as a method of discovery. The pupil would have to think about the question, formulate an answer, and then attempt to defend that answer against the challenge. Dialectic was considered different from rhetoric (Plato) or a counterpart to rhetoric (Aristotle). While rhetoric's primary purpose is persuasion, dialectic's is argument and reason. Law schools still employ the method to some extent so that future attorneys can become accustomed to the adversarial nature of trial law and comprehend the application of statutes and case law to situations. Dialectic of this sort can certainly be employed in undergraduate courses, requiring students to respond to, and constantly to anticipate—a kind of disputation based in logic, reason, evidence, and history. Students introduced to this kind of dialectic can undergo some cognitive changes. They begin to comprehend that thoughts and beliefs, if they are to be held in the face of challenge, must have foundations that resist antithetical confrontation. That is, if a thought is to survive, it should have logic, reason, and evidence on its side, which means that the student who holds the thought should subject it to rigorous scrutiny. A primary benefit is that students may begin to think in terms of questions, and may question their own positions on difficult matters. The skill of engaging in the dialectic has to be taught and practiced; we cannot assume that it is innate. Strategies including active learning are amenable to the dialectical approach; students are in no way passive as they subject thoughts to scrutiny.

Later ideas of dialectic (extending forward from Marx, and addressed by, among others, Paul Ricoeur and Charles Taylor) expand the reasoning that is to be applied to include historical analysis in an attempt to weigh what might be said against a context of change. Understanding of the history of an event or an idea includes awareness of contests that have accompanied the event or idea. Such understanding embraces the multi-vocal past that events and ideas have; it necessitates addressing the disagreement and competition for ascendancy that took place. The version of dialectic that I am speaking of here is more of the sort that incorporates history. The approach requires looking beyond appearances. Examination must begin with perception of the world and of what is said about the world. But we cannot stop there. As Bertell Ollman (2003) points out, the examination has to extend to "the fact that reality is more than appearances and that focusing exclusively on appearances, on the evidence that strikes us immediately and directly, can be extremely misleading.... In a similar way, understanding anything in our everyday experience requires that we know something about how it arose and developed and how it fits into the larger context or system of which it is a part" (p. 13). That is, the critical analysis of something exists in a context of complex social, political, economic, and intellectual dynamics. A dialectical approach to learning, and as much to libraries' instruction programs as anything else, builds upon the information acquisition and synthesis, and development of a knowledge base, that the early years of schooling should achieve. At the point when students are ready—cognitively and psychologically—to deal with contradictions, differences, and disagreements, a dialectical approach can be helpful.

Dialectic provides one way to approach the extremely important process of evaluation. It is essential that the assessment of what others say, write, and show be a component of any instruction, and the ACRL Standards correctly emphasize evaluation. That said, one of the Standards that addresses the evaluation of information could admit to additional guidance for instructors. Frequently instrumental means—author's reputation, peer review practices of a journal, publisher, and others—are applied to evaluation; those means are a necessary means of analysis. Such elements as the source (where the information appears, such a journal), author (qualifications of the person to speak about the topic), and secondary work (who is cited by the author to lend credence to evidence, arguments, and conclusions) can be seen as part of the dialectical approach. As a particular example, evaluation of thought on the topic of intelligent design and evolution cannot be limited to where information appears and who says what; it relies on *what is said*. The aforementioned elements contextualize, to an extent, what is said, but a genuine analysis has to go beyond these elements.

Many ideas are problematic, in that there is disagreement that permeates every part of the idea. Global climate change is a topic that cries for dialectical examination. For one thing, the earth has a history of changes that have taken place and that has left evidence of what has happened. Warmings and coolings have occurred and the events have been studied. There are even more detailed climatological records for the recent past. The data point to some amount of change over the last hundred or so years. The warming phenomenon is studied by means of meteorology, geology, atmospheric chemistry, and others. The question that is raised most often is whether, or to what extent, the warming is caused by anthropogenic (human) sources. That question leads to bodies of evidence, interpretations of evidence, arguments for the legitimacy of some interpretations, and decisions based on the arguments. The question may also be the basis for some assignments that undergraduate students are required to complete, including some in libraries' instructional programs. There is likely to be little argument that students should be able to locate and identify differing views on climate change. But what next; what should students be able to do with that information?

At this point we reach a bridge (metaphorically, but almost literally) in undergraduate student learning. To reiterate, the students should be taught to locate and identify sources of information. An instructional program that fails in this regard fails utterly. This marker is on one side of the bridge. It is here that there is apparent disagreement in the profession; that is, there is a considerable amount of tacit belief that libraries' instructional programs should stay on one side of the bridge, but some argue in favor of crossing it. Student learning is not in dispute, but the nature and degree of learning is the most profound, but tacit, expression of the stay-off-the-bridge position in the very name "information literacy." Chapter Two will address in detail the problems that the name creates; for now we can focus attention on the bridge. Bonnie Gratch Lindauer's (2004) evidence for student outcomes is one guide to the position advocating remaining on one side: "Examples of methods that generate student learning outcomes data include course-imbedded assignments; portfolios of student work scoring rubrics to evaluate them…; research process journals and diaries; pre- and post-tests and quizzes; compilation of anecdotes and learner comments; bibliography analysis; and grades in literacy credit courses" (p. 125). The evaluation criteria she suggests do not step over into analysis (e.g., logical, empirical, rhetorical, or phenomenological) of what people say on a topic; they remain in one particular cognitive domain (the instrumental). A frequent occurrence in professional discourse, mention is made by Lindauer of the possibility of transcending the instrumental manner of learning. Actual transcendence appears to be absent, though. The evaluative standards promulgated by ACRL are an example of the rhetoric of, but not a true argument for, transcendence.

The instrumental component of instruction recurs in the professional literature. Writing for a broad higher education audience, Patricia Senn Breivik (2005) proposes that, "What is growing ever more obvious is that today's undergraduates are generally far less prepared to do research than were students of earlier generations, despite their familiarity with powerful new information-gathering tools" (p. 22). A question that can be asked relates to the extent that familiarity with tools may inhibit students' proficiency in the area of critical inquiry. In a more explicit piece Jill Jensen (2005) suggests a set of questions that students ought to be able to answer:

1. What is the difference among the search options (for example, complex search, advanced search, subject search, and keyword search)? How is each used most effectively? What are the differences in the results?
2. What do the various numerals and letters mean in a citation that looks like this: v274 n5 p366D(1)?
3. Where is the name of the database found? The periodical?
4. Where does the abstract end and the article begin?
5. Why is there a print command on the screen when print is already an option under "File" in the browser's menu bar?
6. Why do the page numbers that the citation says the article is on not match the page numbers that appear when the article is printed?
7. How can I tell what kind of source this is (scholarly journal, weekly periodical, newspaper, and so on) so I can cite it correctly? (p. 112)

This list is, of course, valuable and should be considered for inclusion in courses, but the items are functional, rather than critical. William Orme (2004) also speaks of a program designed to enable students to "perform tasks related to information research" (p. 205). Research is only partly task-based, though. The discussion of librarians' pedagogical content should include Paul Hrycaj's (2006) study in particular. His examination includes the syllabi of 100 credit-bearing library instruction courses and he concludes, "In summary, this study of online syllabi gives qualified support to the author's hypothesis that matters of information access, which are the focus of ACRL Standard Two, are the dominant subject matter of credit-bearing college and university library skills courses.... But the other parts of Standard Three, dealing with critical thinking and information synthesis, did not appear to have much representation in the syllabi" (p. 533).

What of the other side of the bridge? Some librarians do advocate crossing it and engaging the words and thoughts of others actively and critically in libraries' instructional programs. James Elmborg (2006) is one who argues for a richer learning experience for students. He draws from John Dewey in one of his pieces in order to bring home the point that, "Information can stimulate thought, but it should not be confused with thought" (p. 12). The statement sounds like a truism, but it is an essential realization that all educators should keep in mind. Programs exist to transform students' thinking, and the process of learning necessarily includes evaluating the thinking of others. Elmborg points out an advantage of libraries' programs: they are not the narrow province of faculty in particular academic departments, so they have the opportunity to introduce thought from many areas as a means for students to connect ideas in creative ways. Randy Burke Hensley (2006) and Darren Cambridge (2006) illustrate something that may be most important to student learning (and not just in libraries' programs). Information sources—textbooks, journals, items in databases, and Web sites—can seem impersonal to the point that the human agency that expressed the thought may be obscured. Hensley and Cambridge emphasize that learning depends on some active engagement in thought so that students can transcend a passive acceptance of what is said merely because it appears in some "place" (such as a journal, a book, a Web site).

An instrumental approach, explicitly or implicitly, tends to conceive of information as thing. Some years ago Michael Buckland (1991) suggested that there are some distinct ways to think of information. The "object" of information is something that can be managed, stored, retrieved, and manipulated. We can borrow semiotics here (another technical language that can help connect with other fields). In librarianship "information" is a sign; something that we try to invest with meaning, and can be interpreted as having meaning. "Information" consists of the word information itself (the *signifier* in the language of semiotics). It also consists of the concept that the word is to represent (the *signified*) (see Eco 1984). Signs are clearest when the signifier relates in an unambiguous way to one signified. Since there can be unavoidable difficulties (say, one word (signifier) with more than one possible conceptualization (signifieds)), the context in which a sign occurs can help people discern meaning. In applying semiotics, it becomes apparent that the word "information" is a poor signifier for the objective concept; an alternative like "document," although itself somewhat problematic, might be preferable. One does not read a book (unless one is examining a book primarily as a physical object) merely to have flipped through an object made primarily of paper that is spotted with ink. Reading, as Wolfgang Iser (1978) clearly and correctly says, is; that is, reading is itself a phenomenon that is facilitated by an object, but is not simply objective. A challenge that faces the profession is that librarians are free to design instructional programs that are based on any of a number of conceptions of information.

I cannot emphasize enough the importance of transcending thinking of source as thing (looking, for example, as a journal article as something that does nothing than fulfill an assignment requirement). Learning requires a particular kind of worldview to be most effective. Learning, being more than the assimilation of information and the recital of "facts," necessitates an understanding of what is communicated by others. At its most basic, the understanding entails rich communication between teacher and student, and among students. The teacher, rather than presenting only formulae, dates, events, and so on, relates how things came about. The human action that has led to discovery, exploration, warfare, etc. has human origins. A teacher of physics can let students know that there are things in the world that are independent of our minds, observations, and even existence. That teacher can further inform students that the *study* of those natural things is a human endeavor, that someone did examine what occurs, that someone asked questions. The understanding that can arise from such rich communication includes the recognition that inquisitive people have wondered about phenomena and they have tried to explain the phenomena. The explorations have changed over time as people have learned more. People who have helped us all understand some phenomena more clearly started from the same point that students are at now. The transcendence of source as thing is the phenomenological part of phenomenological cognitive action; it puts students (in the broadest sense of the word) on the path to understanding *what* is said.

Phenomenology

I will not pretend that phenomenology is a simple idea, but I will maintain that it is not merely part of academic jargon and obfuscation. As is true of almost all philosophical positions, phenomenology has several forms, described by a number of people. What fits education best is a hybrid version. That said, there are some consistently held elements in the various conceptions of phenomenology. For one thing, phenomenology is an exercise of reasoning; it is a process of examination. That includes the intentionality that underlies most human action. That is, people do things, say things, and think things on purpose; they *mean* to engage in the action. Intentionality is rather elusive at times, though. For example, I may say global climate change is a myth, not because I believe there is no basis or evidence for climate change, but because I believe that policies directed at slowing, stopping, or reversing climate change are contrary to certain of my interests. Edmund Husserl (1859-1938), perhaps the foremost pioneer of phenomenology, maintains that we refrain from presupposing anything. In the example just given, what would be required is to investigate *why* I would make such a claim about climate change. If the reasons for my intentional stance are not linked to the phenomenon of climate change, the investigator's challenge is to uncover what *are* the reasons for my stance. For Husserl, this kind of investigation is the necessary first step. Whether it should come first or not is debatable, but it is vital to learning.

Another common (and key) element of phenomenology is the concept of lifeworld (*lebenswelt* for Husserl, Heidegger, and others). Lifeworld is at once an individual and a shared concept. Each of us has a set of experiences, beliefs, and perceptions of the world that contributes to shaping our underlying view of what exists. There is a degree to which that set that an individual has may be a product of the experiences and beliefs of a group. Family, town, church, school, political party, and other affiliations can affect the lifeworld. In phenomenology the set of experiences, beliefs, and perceptions both provides a background to what we experience *and* constitutes something to be examined. Lifeworld (as Husserl began to use it in *Ideas I*, 1913), then, is a complex kind of subjectivity; it is a lens through which each of us gazes and it is also potentially a blinder that may obscure perception. The process of learning requires comprehending the complexity. Lifeworld is not a suit of armor that we cannot escape; it is a fluid and changing frame that enables each of us to grasp the world we live in. The lifeworld is intersubjective as well; our interactions with one another can challenge our perceptions. Education, as a component of lifeworld, necessitates making the lifeworld explicit. Discussions in class and reading and seeing what others say can expand and alter individuals' lifeworlds. The change that is possible depends on a combination of the observer-independent world (such as a mountain or a lake) and the observer-dependent world (such as the meaning of a poem), especially human action that can be interpreted in multiple ways.

Both intentionality and lifeworld point to an aspect of phenomenology that more recent thinkers (such as Heidegger, Sartre, Merleau-Ponty, and Ricoeur) have added—the relationship of self and other (sometimes expressed as I and Thou). This aspect is by no means reducible to differences, although differences do exist. You and I may disagree; we may believe in conflicting ideas. Phenomenology demands that I do not dismiss your beliefs simply because they are not the same as mine. I have the responsibility to examine your belief or opinion and why you hold it. You embody intentionality just as much as I do; you have your lifeworld, just as I do. What Husserl's version of phenomenology requires is that I do not accept what you say on the sole basis of your intentionality and lifeworld; Husserl's imperative is emphasized by Paul Ricoeur and Emmanuel Levinas in all of their writings. I have to assess what you say according to evidentiary thought as well (empirical, logical, and other justification for what you say). What this means is that I can (and must) evaluate what you say as part of your experiences and perceptions, but also as part of a larger, communicated, set of experiences, perceptions, and statements of many people. If you say that everyone has a moral obligation to try to stop global climate change, I must assess your statement according to a moral framework that is part of your lifeworld, the physical evidence for climate change, the policy alternatives that others articulate, and my own moral framework. Engaging in this kind of analysis not only helps me understand your statement; it helps me evaluate where I stand on the matter. Education is more than an agglomeration of experiences of selves; it is an engagement of selves (of I and Thou).

Undergraduate students are not very likely to have a clear understanding of phenomenology and may not pay a great deal of attention to the tenets of phenomenology in a library's instructional program. Fortunately, phenomenology can be presented by examples and through application, rather than as an abstract philosophical principle. There are some ways to use some of the intuitions that students have as a way of bringing home some of the ideas. For example, as students retrieve items from the library's catalog or a database they can be reminded that the author(s) of the item created the work to communicate intentionally with an audience. The author(s) is trying to share thought or research and is trying to be understood by readers. As an exercise, each student could be asked to tell another student something about herself or himself, her or his major, her or his plans after college. The communicating student can be asked how she or he chose what to tell and how to tell it, to think about her or his own intentionality. The exercise can also be used to narrow any distance between the students and the authors of retrieved items. The conversation among students, and the discussion between the teacher and the students, can be compared to reading the authors' works. Since students may take advantage of such tools as MySpace and YouTube, those can also be used to illustrate mediated conversation. (More on this type of exercise will be said in the chapter on the example of course content.)

One thing can be said about this type of exercise here, as a way to introduce a somewhat different framework for understanding students' uses of information. That is, in examining the place of libraries' programs in communicating about knowledge production Shilpa Shanbhaq (2006) says, "Students function not only within their immediate environment, such as the library or the academy, but also within a larger society. Here, they come across as many meanings of knowledge, research, information, and truth as ways to achieve them" (p. 3). Shanbhaq further states that information literacy is more akin to a liberal art than to a cluster of skills. That distinction is important. Shanbhaq draws from an idea proposed by Jeremy Shapiro and Shelley Hughes (1996), who state that information literacy is "the critical reflection on the nature of information itself, its technical infrastructure and its social, cultural and even philosophical context and impact." There is a sense in which Shapiro and Hughes's idea is correct and useful, and a sense in which it obscures a fundamental aspect of learning; the latter being a focus that be too heavy on the technical infrastructure. The correct sense (the context and impact) can, and should, be a component of every instructional program, since it helps illustrate the differing lifeworlds that people have. One's lifeworld will influence the framework according to which the person asks a question. Gender, race, and ethnicity (among other things) are parts of a person's lifeworld, so a particular issue might be perceived from the standpoint of, say, an African-American woman. The standpoint is not likely to be absolute, otherwise communication across genders, races, etc. would be impossible. Moreover, a phenomenological stance can prevent communicative limitations based on difference if one does indeed accommodate both I and Thou. The obscurantist sense follows from the realization that *what* informs (literally, what gives shape and form) is more than information as thing or technology. What informs is what speaks to someone; it is what is said and heard. Any exercise aimed at identifying "books," "scholarship," or "popular literature" (for its own sake or in isolation from *what* is communicated) is meaningless. Understanding tools is very important, but only inasmuch as tools enable people to *do* something.

Students in libraries' instructional programs are not likely to be interested in information *as* information (information as an ill-defined thing). Students are also not likely to retrieve the scores of football games as a way to test a particular number theory; they will want to know which teams won and which teams lost. John Doherty and Kevin Ketchner (2005) borrow from Paolo Freire (1970) to explain that the purposes of many of our practices, from the reference interview to bibliographic instruction, force students to come to us on our terms, to meet our goals and our agendas. Instead, we should value and build on the experiences of students" (p. 8). Students' own terms frequently relate to the work they do in all of the courses they take. Successful completion of assignments, satisfactory performance in courses, and learning are most probably going to be their goals. Put another way, the location of information and the manipulation of information resources are not, for the students, domain-specific knowledge and learning events. The contextualization of the work within a broad education and learning arena is likely to be more effective than looking at works in isolation (see, for example, Matthews, 2000).

This is an opportune time to return to dialectics. Phenomenology and dialectics are not usually connected but, as I hope to show, the common elements of phenomenology are amenable to a dialectical approach to learning and knowledge. One shared goal between the two is progressing to knowledge from opinion (what Plato and Aristotle said was achieving *epistēmē* (knowledge) as opposed to just *doxa* (opinion)). The entirety of phenomenological cognitive action is premised on an anti-positivist foundation (to put the framework in academic-speak). To couch this idea in a more accessible way, phenomenological cognitive action exists within, and contrary to, a particular philosophical tradition. At the heart of positivism is the presumption that we can be certain of some things (positivists would say that we can verify claims and statements). We gain this certainty through empirical means—direct observation—and logical means—applying strict rules to the analysis of statements. One positivist objective is the discovery of laws that can explain and predict phenomena. For example, Carl Gustav Hempel (2001) argued that we can derive laws of history. In the natural sciences positivism was dealt serious blows in the early twentieth century by relativity and quantum mechanics, both of which demonstrate the problem associated with achieving certainty. Later in the century the social sciences began to abandon positivism; the failure to find covering laws for psychological, social, or political behavior was determined to be, not merely elusive, but impossible. The behaviorism of John Watson and B. F. Skinner was an experiment in positivism that psychologists have, for the most part, drifted away from. Positivism, as a way of thinking, suppresses any historical situatedness and application of reasoning that are necessary to learning (Toulmin, 2001).

Recognizing that positivism is an impoverished way of thinking, we can look to other positions, such as phenomenology, to try to understand human action. One of positivism's shortcomings is that it admits only a material reality (for instance, only what is physically real can be experienced by the senses). Phenomenology is built on a realization that reality is simultaneously materialist, subjective, and intersubjective. What this means is that each of us perceives something real (and thoughts and ideas are real) by means of our individual experiences and beliefs, which are influenced by our relationships with others. The difference between positivism and phenomenology is vitally important to education. According to positivism, only concrete sensations and rules of logic can be part of teaching and learning. Phenomenology accepts that sensations and logic are part of the educational process, but those two things alone do not help us comprehend phenomena such as war, poverty, social affiliation, political action, etc. Those phenomena are products of material reality, along with our own individual beliefs and knowledge, and the collective experiences and knowledge claims of groups. The subjective and intersubjective elements are grounds for conflict, dispute, contradiction, competing theses, and so on. That such contests exist cannot be denied; their existence suggests challenges for education (and for knowledge itself).

Introducing Dialectic

The kind of educational approach I am advocating here is described by Roslyn Wallach Bologh (1979): "Instead of assuming that an object's meaning or sense is inherent or given with the object, phenomenology claims that we can know the meaning or sense of an object only in its relation to a knowing subject. The meaning is grounded in or internal to the relation of subject and object. It is not internal to the object, nor is it internal to the subject. This approach is in its nature dialectical" (p. 2). What Bologh is suggesting is that both objectivity and subjectivity exist, that there is tension between the two, and that an intellectual struggle is the only means to reconciliation. Bologh's formulation of dialectical phenomenology is a direct result of her study of Karl Marx's political economy. According to Marx's thesis (expressed throughout his economic writings), labor—which is subjective in that it is an action undertaken by people—is completely objectified in terms of commodity production. The value of labor, then, exists in terms of the exchange value of the commodities that are produced. I use her example of Marx deliberately here for two reasons. The first is that education as a whole in the U.S. today is taking the kind of objectifying turn that much of society, through capitalism, took a few centuries ago. The second is that libraries' instructional programs, insofar as they have emphasized information as thing over the understanding of the communicative action that is essential to knowledge growth, has been an objectifying force as well. Both of these reasons require more explanation.

The first reason is based on observations and evidence provided by numerous people who study higher education. Criticisms include those of Jean-François Lyotard (1984), who warns against commodifying education. Lyotard is an avowed postmodernist; the locus for legitimacy of some thing we take for granted (such as science) is language. The linguistic element, for him, is *the* shaper of meaning, but there are pessimistic implications for shifts in meaning. He writes, ""Knowledge is and will be produced in order to be sold, it is and will be consumed in order to be valorized in a new production: in both cases the goal is exchange. Knowledge ceases to be an end in itself; it loses its 'use-value'" (p. 4). More recently Derek Bok (2003) has written of the growing commercialization of higher education in many ways. State support for public colleges and universities has been shrinking in the last several years, necessitating that institutions explore other source of revenue or to cut costs. Some commentators, such as Richard Kent Vedder (2004), have suggested, in keeping with commodifying education, that increases in teaching loads and larger class sizes are needed responses to higher education's dilemma. If money is the sole measure, then this kind of response makes sense; if learning is the objective, though, the response is incoherent. The purpose here is not to enter into a prolonged critique of higher education financing. The evidence presented does suggest that the fiscal constraints under which colleges and universities operate contribute to what has been called a neoliberal direction higher education. "Neoliberalism" refers to freedom of markets, wherein freedom is achieved when transactions are maximized. As Lyotard warns, everything, including education, can be transformed into monetary transactions. (See Budd, 2009, for a more extensive discussion of capital and higher education.)

The example of Marx (even if it does not lead to a typically Marxist standpoint on such matters as class and labor) provides a context for examination of the state of higher education today. It is only speculation, but if students of two centuries ago were asked why they were attending college, at least some portion of them may have responded that they were seeking to learn more. The economic return on education was not great (and the students were likely to be from the upper classes), so that pull would not likely have been enticing. Today the economic impact that a bachelor's degree can make is substantial; that may be the principal reason why many people attend college today. It is also an open question to what extent the students of two centuries ago might have identified themselves through their educations. That is, graduation from a college may have been a portion of attributes according to which a person would conceive of self and self-in-the-world. With slight economic differences at stake, the distinction was likely to be largely subjective, part of self-identification. As education (in the sense of degrees earned) increasingly acquired a material character, "being educated" signaled a shift from having a subjective character to having an objective one. At this point in time colleges and universities face an uphill climb if they want to recapture the subjective element of education. This is the environment in which instructional programs exist.

The second reason for using the example of Marx gets to the heart of this book. Practices that revolve around the demonstration of resources carry the danger of elevating resources beyond their function as tools. There is no question that many instructional programs transcend the material, but there is also no question that the professional discourse contains quite a lot of emphasis on information as thing. As far back as 1989 the ALA Presidential Committee on Information Literacy stated, "To be information literate, a person must be able to recognize when information is needed and have the ability to locate, evaluate, and use effectively the needed information." Bill Johnston and Sheila Webber (2003), commenting on the definition, say, "Notable is the emphasis on recognising an information need, evaluating what is found, and using the information effectively. This already distinguishes it from descriptions of 'information search' or 'information finding', which foreground the information location element of information literacy. Also notable is the way the definition is made not be mapping a subject area, but via a description of personal skills" (p. 337). Elmborg (2006) does not mince words: "By objectifying and decontextualizing phenomena in the search for broad structural patterns, information literacy researchers have separated students from social and economic contexts, thereby detaching them from school, teacher, and society in an effort to isolate variables to create more pure 'scientific' studies" (p. 194). In addition to the social and economic contexts, intellectual domains, cognitive states, and relationships with the vast bodies of thought also stress the material, subjective, and intersubjective elements. The ALA definition, and the ACRL Standards, are very influential, so the context of the statements requires careful scrutiny.

Learning Theory—Constructivism

As we travel beyond the merely material and incorporate the subjective and intersubjective, we run head-on into some serious challenges. A major challenge centers on how people learn and what knowledge is.

This challenge to all of education has been examined, debated, disputed, and contested for a number of years. Some labels have been applied to some of the ways of thinking about learning and knowledge; one of these is constructivism. No surprises here; constructivism means many things to different people. One definition of constructivism is offered by Vivien Burr (2003): "Forms of psychology that see the person as having an active role in the creation of their experience; each person perceives the world differently and creates their own meanings from events" (p. 201). This definition underscores some of the conceptual problems of the label. The first part is indispensable; thinking, learning, and knowing require action by individuals. Experience, reasoning, and other means come into play as people develop ideas about themselves and the world around them. An educational corollary to the first part of the definition holds that teachers have the responsibility to support students' construction of knowledge not just from experience, but also from testimony, argument, etc. On the face of it, there is no problem with constructivism so simply stated. As we delve a bit deeper, though, we see that questions rear their heads, and that we cannot avoid addressing them. The exploration is necessary because this theory is prominent in education today.

Constructivism, as it is discussed by many people, has a tendency to subvert the material. If a premise is that each of us constructs a world, then the subjective aspect dominates. Ernst von Glasersfeld (1995) articulates a very strong version of constructivism that is consistent with the second part of Burr's definition: "What is radical constructivism? It is an unconventional approach to the problem of knowledge and knowing. It starts from the assumption that knowledge, no matter how it is defined, is the heads of persons, and that the thinking subject has no alternative but to construct what he or she knows on the basis of his or her own experience" (p. 1). He denies that this strong version descends into solipsism (the idea that only "I" exist, and everything, including other people, are "my" creations), but the danger is real. The radical version of constructivism, rather than being a theory of knowledge, is a denial of epistemology. If each individual separately constructs a world from individual experience, then agreement on aspects of the world is purely accidental (converging, at best, only as experiences are shared). Von Glasersfeld (1995) says, "Radical constructivism is uninhibitedly instrumentalist. It replaces the notion of 'truth' (as true representations of an independent reality) with the notion of 'viability' within the subjects' experiential world. Consequently it refuses all metaphysical commitments and claims to be no more than one possible model of thinking about the only world we can know, the world we construct as living subjects" (p. 22). Instrumentalism is also problematic, especially if "viability" is individually constructed. Of necessity, it is not only truth that is abandoned, but also ethics, since there is no reason to recognize another person as another self. This conclusion is inescapable if we accept von Glasersfeld's contention that, "from the constructivist perspective, knowledge does not constitute a 'picture' of the world. It does not represent the world at all—it comprises action schemes, concepts, and thoughts, and it distinguishes the ones that are considered advantageous from those that are not" (p. 114). Von Glasersfeld's idea is self defeating. What is advantageous, what comprises an action scheme, depends on what *is*. Physical laws describe the world in certain specific and real ways that we have to heed if we want to succeed, and even survive. We do construct some ways of thinking about the world, but it is foolish to believe that our thinking about the world is not influenced by the world itself.

Another version of constructivism emphasizes intersubjectivity. The social version can be radical as well. Burr (2003) maintains, "Our ways of understanding the world do not come from objective reality but from other people, both past and present" (p. 7), and argues that, "If our knowledge of the world, our common ways of understanding it, is not derived from the nature of the world as it really is, where does it come from? The social constructionist answer is that people construct it between them" (p. 4). This version is as problematic as von Glasersfeld's. For example, Barbara Hernstein Smith (2005) says, "As distinct from rationalist conceptualisations, knowledge (everyday, expert, or scientific) may be understood not in opposition to ('mere') belief but as beliefs that have become relatively well established" (p. 11). General cognitive processes include reasoning, so if beliefs do become established, they do so by some process that includes reasoning. In the extreme, and Smith represents an extreme view, social constructivism is opposed to science as a rational endeavor in many ways. In agreeing with Ludvik Fleck, Smith (2005) is of the opinion that, "the scientist's perceptions of the physical world are no more objective than those of anyone else since, like anyone else's they are shaped by a particular experiential history in a particular social-epistemic community" (p. 27). This statement can only be coherent if one believes that there is no mind- or observer-independent world. It takes very little intellectual skill (calling, for example, on the application of some scientific laws) to demonstrate that the idea is foolish. The folly can be confirmed by using some ideas to illustrate the errors of their authors. Nelson Goodman (1978) used constellations as evidence that people create stars. It is completely reasonable to say that people represent particular images (Orion, for instance) by drawing boundaries around stars, but the stars themselves exist for the boundaries to be drawn.

I have endeavored to demonstrate flaws of strong versions of constructivism as a way to confirm positive and useful elements of weaker versions. A weak version is one component of an epistemological—and pedagogical—program that necessarily includes the material, subjective, and intersubjective elements. The subjective and intersubjective aspects are the focus of the construction of knowledge. Individuals, in some kind of cooperation with other individuals, work within systems of awareness, understanding, and knowledge to incorporate the ideas, images, and thoughts they experience. One mechanism that people use to learn is locating analogues. A new experience is *like* a familiar one in key ways; there are points of similarity that can be observed, as well as points of difference. Whether explicit or not, categorization helps people find analogous experiences. There may be similarities of size, color, movement, but also of reference (in the sense of drawing from familiar premises), content (topical similarities), and other things. The intersubjective elements, particularly in a classroom, can allow individuals to communicate the background (the points that begin the search for analogues). The introduction of categorization explicitly in the classroom is essential to libraries' instruction programs. Mechanisms like the search for analogues foster the construction of knowledge. Still, the construction has its building materials, which are the material components. The combination of the three components—material, subjective, and intersubjective—provides us with a pedagogical foundation that we can use to develop effective courses.

The weaker version of constructivism is open to incorporating components of other theories of knowledge. In other words, it is not intended to stand completely alone and does not fall prey to a mistaken competitive refutation of all other theories. The weaker version is concerned with action, including the demonstration that students have the capability to *do* something. The action-related aspect of learning has to be considered very carefully. It would be easy for instructors who reduce teaching and learning to the presentation and quasi-functional manipulation of resources to claiming that students know something because of their completion of some assignments. "Quasi-functional" is my term of choice here because, in a reductionist experience, the real function of contemplating what others say is lost. Most importantly, constructivism (weak or strong) is not likely to be an instructional design technique. The weak version actually amounts to a learning objective—enabling students to build upon their experiences, their present knowledge base, and cognitive state seems to help them gain a broader and/or deeper understanding of some phenomena (Jonassen, 2006). As an epistemological position, constructivism is agnostic when it comes to the *content* of knowledge claims. The weak version, however, is compatible with normative epistemological requirements, including justification and warrant. In fact, normative (stated as prescriptive, or the way things should be) criteria, it can be argued, are necessary for learning. The process of evaluation, in conjunction with intellectual integrity, is essential for undergraduate student learning.

The foregoing defense of weak constructivism raises a few more concerns for libraries' instructional programs. The primary concern relates to the content of the programs. Several years ago Rachel Naismith and Joan Stein (1989) examined what might be called the linguistic competence of students in a course. Their testing centered on students' comprehension of some of the technical language of librarianship. They found that the students did not have the ability to interpret the technical definitions of words that have other referential meaning (including "reference" and "citation"). The lesson to be learned from their work is extremely important, not just because it points to a need for vocabulary training, but because it indicates something about cognition and undergraduate students. We could say that the technical language of librarianship reflects the domain of the profession, or we could say that the language is not domain-specific; for the purposes of instructional programs the choice does not matter (ultimately it does matter to the profession). The technical language that librarians use is not likely to fit into any domain (art, history, chemistry, etc.) that students are aware of. In other words, the students are not able to see the language as in any referential (connected to specific meanings). Moreover, the language is pertinent to the domain-specific knowledge and needs of students only insofar as it serves as a means to enhancing their ability to assess and incorporate the thought and ideas of others in fields that hold their interest.

Learning Theory—Social Epistemology

A weak version of constructivism is also consistent with social epistemology. Social epistemology is not usually categorized as a learning theory, but it is very helpful as a tool to help us think about learning. The concept of social epistemology comes from our own field. More than half a century ago Margaret Egan and Jesse Shera (1952) used the term to refer to "a system of "production, distribution, and utilization of intellectual products...." Social epistemology has been used more recently by philosophers; Steve Fuller (1988) says that the idea begins with a question: "How should the pursuit of knowledge be organized, given that under normal circumstances knowledge is pursued by many human beings, each working on a more or less well-defined body of knowledge and each equipped with roughly the same imperfect cognitive capacities, albeit with varying degree of access to one another's activities" (p. 3)? That question is not only interesting; it is quite useful in the consideration of libraries' instructional programs. It captures the state of the students in a class *and* their relationship to the work that others have done. There are some limitations to that question, though. It does not address the rich possibilities for knowledge growth *by individuals, socially situated.*

The work of Alvin Goldman (1999, 2002) provides the most thorough explanation of the possibilities of social epistemology. As a path to seeking truth, social epistemology can open both investigative possibilities and pedagogical opportunities.

> In what respects is social epistemology social? First, it focuses on social paths or routes to knowledge. That is, considering believers taken one at a time, it looks at the many routes to belief that feature interactions with other agents, as contrasted with private and asocial routes to belief acquisition.... Second, social epistemology does not restrict itself to believers taken

singly. It often focuses on some sort of group entity—a
team of co-workers, a set of voters in a political juris-
diction, or an entire society—and examines the spread
of information or misinformation across that group's
membership.... Third, instead of restricting knowers to
individuals, social epistemology may consider collective or corporate entities, such as juries or legislatures,
as potential knowing agents (Goldman, 1999, pp. 4-5)

The classroom is itself a social path to knowledge; in it there can
be discourse, interrogation, argumentation, conjecture, as well as the
normative element, which is prominent in the goal of seeking truth.
The very idea of truth necessitates a normative stance, which is what
Goldman calls veritism. According to him, social epistemology, "has
the distinctive normative purpose of evaluating or appraising [social
practices] on the vertistic dimension, that is, in terms of their respective
knowledge consequences" (Goldman, 1999, p, 6). One attractive part of
social epistemology is its rootedness in the real world; it is concerned
with genuine human action and it offers concrete suggestions that can
be integrated into education. For instance, Goldman (2002) presents
details on the means that can be employed to assess what experts say,
including comparing statements by various experts. This applies directly
to the teacher-student relationship and students' readings that are assigned or found as part of course work (pp. 139-63).

There is one more feature of social epistemology that affirms its usefulness in education in general and libraries' instructional programs in
particular. In addition to providing norms for truth seeking as a social
phenomenon, it also points to cognitive processes that can and should
be developed as part of learning. Hilary Kornblith (1994) expresses the
feature clearly: "the main social epistemological project consists in the
investigation of the reliability of various types of social processes. Once
we have recognized that individuals form beliefs by relying on information supplied by others, there are serious issues about the conditions that
should be met if the community is to form a consensus on a particular
issue" (p. 114). When veritism (searching for the truth of statements) and
reliabilism (assessing the reliability, or coherence with known things,
of claims) are combined, the goals and processes of knowledge growth
are clarified. Libraries' instructional programs exist to provide students

with the wherewithal to learn from what others say and show. Social epistemology, then, can be a centerpiece of courses. The dynamism of social epistemology will be explored further as discussion in turns to course design and evaluation.

Categorization

The use of language and the possibilities of language call to mind a very important component of instruction and of seeking and finding information—categorization. Categorization is at once indispensable and problematic. John Searle (1995) warns, "Any system of classification or individuation of objects, any set of categories for describing the world, indeed, any system of representation at all is conventional, and to that extent arbitrary" (p. 160). If categorization is arbitrary, are we up against a hopeless task? Is there any way to design an instructional program in which categorization features prominently? There is no cause for despair; as a society we address the challenge constantly and we constantly come up with solutions. One of Searle's favorite examples is money, which is just such a social creation. The physical substance of pieces of paper or metal does not constitute money; our collective and institutional (in the case of money, the federal government) acceptance constitutes money. Based on the agreement we can categorize very specific pieces of paper and metal as money. We do not have to teach freshmen what money is because the collective and institutional reality is something they have already accepted and used. In fact, if we were to use money as an example in a class we have to explain *how* it is a collective and institutional reality that is not questioned.

The example of money is one instance of an argument that Searle (1995) presents: "Premise: Any cognitive state occurs as part of a set of cognitive states and within a cognitive system…. Conclusion 1: It is impossible to get outside of all cognitive states and systems to survey the relationships between them and the reality that they are used to cognize" (p. 174). In short, Searle maintains that, for each of us, the present cognitive state has been shaped by the cognitive states of others (including institutions), and that each of us is bound by a cognitive state (since the state is, to a considerable extent, constitutive of us). This sounds complicated, so let us take it in steps. My own present cognitive state has been formed by my parents, my schooling, my living in the United States, what I have read and heard, and many other factors, *including my own assessment of consistencies and inconsistencies in those background facts.* My cognitive state did not somehow spring full blown. Because of the influences and their complexities and subtleties I cannot stand outside myself to examine why I think the way I do about the things I think about. By extension, a teacher can in no way demand that a student stand outside himself or herself to examine individual cognitive states. The teacher, further, cannot presume cognitive states that do not exist. That is, the teacher will not succeed, and students will not learn, if the expectation is that there is an "ideal student cognitive state" that is not likely to exist. On the other hand, the class (and by that I mean the teacher, the other students, the syllabus, the readings, the discussions, etc.) influences each student's cognitive state.

Of necessity effective communication is vital to the success of instructional programs. Following from the findings of Naismith and Stein, effective communication relies on what we can call intelligibility (the ability of all in the class to comprehend what is being said). As is the case with domain-specific fields, some vocabulary training will be necessary. Professional librarians will probably be the instructors in the courses, so it is incumbent on them to keep the purpose of the instructional program in mind. It is very easy for an individual to speak in terms that she or he is familiar and comfortable with, but the language may not be entirely shared by undergraduate students. The purpose of the course—to enable students to consider and evaluate the thoughts and ideas of others—requires closing the linguistic gap. A corollary of the purpose is to assist students in the pursuit of knowledge and truth. Michael Luntley (1995) eloquently points out the danger associated with forgetting the purpose: "if we acknowledge the possibility of incommensurable languages, then the pursuit of truth and knowledge is lost. If we acknowledge the idea that there can be interminable disagreements about the very language in which we are to describe experience, language is no longer a medium for investigating something beyond" (p. 98).

The above discussion of language and its centrality to education marks an illustration of the need for a weak constructivist position. As Searle points out, some constructed concepts become so ingrained that they have an objective reality; on the other hand (as Naismith and Stein (1989) demonstrate), there are many concepts that either are not so ingrained or have multiple common meanings. The examples of classification, as will be shown in a later chapter, provide a solid grounding for demonstration of the challenges that language offers. Within librarianship there can be a tendency to treat categories—primarily in the form of subject headings, but also with classification—almost literally as names. In the strictest sense (this strict sense is actually not very useful, though), names denote; they provide a single and complete description of the identity of something. Names can be a more effective concept if Saul Kripke's (1980) looser usage is remembered: "What we really associate with the name is a family of descriptions" (p. 31). The process of education constantly employs mechanisms of signification; that is, language is used so as to connect a word (name or term) with something the word stands for. Libraries' instructional programs, as much as or even more than, any other area of study, makes use of such sign systems. Instruction, therefore, can be more effective if instructors understand the systems as clearly as possible and can transmit that understanding to students.

Onward

To jump ahead, assessment of libraries' instruction programs is an immediate and necessary concern. Bonnie Gratch Lindauer (2004) graphically depicts the interrelated elements of the learning environment, in formal program requirements, and student learning outcomes in one examination of assessment. She does mention, though, that learning outcomes have been influenced by accreditation and other standards. One could question whether accredited should, in itself, ever have been a determining factor of these, or any other, instructional programs. In many instances standards have been designed for application across myriad types of institutions and, in the past, have been prescriptive as to inputs and outputs. Accreditation standards have changed greatly in recent years, in part because they *are* intended to apply to such a variety of institutional types. Lindauer's work is by no means the only one on assessment, but it does raise the issue of external forces that are bound to affect higher education in general. U.S. Secretary of Education Margaret Spellings (see "A Test of Leadership," 2006) has raised skepticism regarding the efficiency of accreditation; it could be that a policy shift will alter the evaluation of all higher education institutions. At the present time the state of policy is in some disarray. Public colleges and universities are funded, to a considerable extent, by states, so state legislatures hold purse strings. The federal government is, at the time of this writing, more activist in higher education policy than it has been for some time. Every institution has to serve multiple constituencies and must address various fiscal challenges. An intended result of an instructional program is raising the consciousnesses of the students, according to the material/subjective/intersubjective conception of consciousness. I have suggested here in the above ideas, taken together, a new framework for instruction.

KEY POINTS IN CHAPTER ONE:

> I intend in this book to offer a framework within which libraries' instructional program can be built—phenomenological cognitive action:

- Phenomenology—the intersubjective relationship of students' intentional search for understanding through the statements, images, or voices of others, and the teachers' engagement of students in those searches
- Cognition—students' ways of thinking about the academic (primarily) challenges they face (through their assignments, papers they write, and explorations they undertake in all of their course work), and also the introduction of metacognitive processes that can help them respond to the challenges
- Action—the students' direct interaction with complex discourse (what others write, say, and show), and the resources that can help them locate the discourse

> Cognition is complex; the cognitive state of undergraduate is even more complex, but understanding it is vital to effective instruction

> An aspect of phenomenology—lifeworld—can help librarians better understand the social, personal, familial, religious, economic, and intersubjective influences on undergraduate students lives

> Education should embody dialectic, which necessarily involves students being active in their learning, as well as in the critical and historical evaluation of what is presented to them

> Social epistemology is one way of locating the educational search for knowledge and truth within intersubjective perceptions of what others write, say, and show

◆

CHAPTER TWO

Beyond Information Literacy

Throughout the first chapter I primarily used the term "libraries' instructional programs." "Information literacy" is more commonly used, but it is problematic to the point that it is not an apt name for a program that would be based on the framework proposed here. If it were simply a matter of a name, discussion could proceed. It is more than that, though. This chapter will take issue, not just with the name, but with the skill- and competency-oriented foundations of many of the official positions on instruction. For example, a thorough examination of the ACRL Standards, according to the proposed framework, will reveal some conceptual and practical difficulties. Of course the Standards do not constitute the first or only instance of the name information literacy. As was mentioned in Chapter One, an ALA Presidential Committee defined information literacy in 1989 (I will return to the Committee's report shortly). More recently, though not marking an advance in language, the Educational Testing Service (ETS) has formulated a position on what it refers to as "Information and Communication Technology (ICT) Proficiencies." The ETS position can be a place to begin investigation into the current state of official thinking about instruction.

ETS Enters the Fray

As was just stated, ETS's entry into the deliberations on information-related skills has been recent. A few years ago ETS convened a panel for the express purpose of studying the role of ICTs in general literacy. Intended to be an international group, only two of the nine panelists resided outside the United States. The panel reported in 2002. In their report the panel wrote, "The panel strongly believes that it is time to expand the notion of the digital divide. The current global public policy focus is on the detrimental impact of limited access to hardware, software and networks such as the Internet. We believe this characterization of the digital divide must be changed to include the impact of limited reading, numeracy, and problem-solving skills. Without these skills, all the hardware and access in the world will not enable people to become ICT literate" (p. 1). It appears that the intentions of the panel are noble; the thinking that is evident in the statement, however, raises some questions. In order to establish the context for the report the panel defines ICT literacy: "ICT literacy is using digital technology, communications tools, and/or networks to access, manage, integrate, evaluate, and create information in order to function in a knowledge society" (p. 2). The definition, along with the position on the digital divide, points to the possibility of developing tests and measures, but those tests and measures could be worse than failure. A failure connotes effort that is clearly directed and goal-driven, but that falls short in some ways. The definition, however, suggests an agenda that is so mired in instrumentalism as to be meaningless. For example, beginning with a premise that people need to be able to use tools utterly misses the point that people employ tools in order to accomplish some particular ends. It should be noted that no librarians were on the ETS panel.

Another ETS publication (2005) proposes components of ICT proficiencies. These are almost identical (with no attribution) to the "Big-6" developed by Michael Eisenberg and Robert Berkowitz. Anyone interested in the Big-6 model should consult Eisenberg and Berkowitz (1990); the conceptual underpinnings are much more fully developed there. The ETS paper does very little, either to define information literacy or to suggest a procedural model for implementing a program. A more recent ETS position paper repeats the model, citing only earlier ETS reports. Given the thrust of evaluation and critical use of information that almost all writings on the topic feature, the ETS report writers appear to lack diligence when it comes to acknowledging work done in information literacy. An alternative interpretation of ETS's paper could be less generous. In the most recent paper the author of the report wrote,

> Ben, my son in the third grade, is participating in an "artifact box" project at his school. For the past several weeks, he and his teammates crafted clues—photos, word puzzles and elided newspaper headlines—that reveal the team's state, town and school. They just

traded boxes with another school and are researching those students' clues. One is a picture of a bird; a quick visit to a teacher-suggested Web site reveals that it is the state bird of Idaho. Others similarly point to Idaho and are all revealed via searches of selected Web sites and, when all else fails, Google (2005, p. 2).

The author ignores the fact that useful print sources may have been able to assist the students. On the whole, the ETS resources simultaneously do not capture the purpose of instruction and rather arrogantly appropriate solutions proposed by others some time ago. The ETS agenda is to treat ICT literacy as an intellectual domain of it own (2002, pp. 17-21). Two assumptions underlie the agenda: (1) ICT literacy is a separate and unique intellectual area, and (2) one single set of skills can enable learners to assimilate what is written, said, and shown across all fields. Since ETS is itself a formidable organization, what it proposes cannot be ignored. Their report, however, can and should be dismissed because of their serious weaknesses.

Defining Information Literacy

Programs, initiatives, and agendas formulated by librarians are more coherent and well conceived than ETS's. That said, official statements and standards in librarianship also warrant critical attention. As was mentioned in Chapter One and above, in 1989 an ALA Presidential Committee reported. The Committee was formed in 1987 by then-ALA President Margaret Chisholm. It had a fairly broad portfolio, and it addressed the needs of people of all ages across a wide range of environments. There are a few specific features of the Committee's final report that articulated some ideas about this information landscape and the challenges it represents. The report (1989) begins, "No other change in American society has offered greater challenges than the emergence of the Information Age." The term Information Age is not defined; it is in fact an elusive and variably described notion. The quantity and, in particular, accessibility of information has certainly prompted changes, but the hyperbole inherent in the statement does not represent the present state very well. For one thing, there have been many developments and events in the nation's and the world's past that have affected people profoundly. For another, the statement paints a picture that includes primarily "stuff;" missing is an admission that people are likely to want to know or be able to do particular things at particular times. The majority of the "stuff" is irrelevant to those kinds of needs, so the challenge presented, especially to librarianship, is not merely a technical one of storage and retrieval.

The report also addresses the importance of people being informed to the growth of a democratic society. The quantity and fragmentation of available information does indeed signal a challenge. The Committee expresses one component of the challenge thusly:

> It is unfortunate that the very people who most need the empowerment inherent in being information literate are the least likely to have learning experiences which will promote these abilities. Minority and at-risk students, illiterate adults, people with English as a second language, and economically disadvantaged people are among those most likely to lack access to the information that can improve their situations. Most are not even aware of the potential help that is available to them. Libraries, which provide the best access point to information for most U.S. citizens, are left untapped by those who most need help to improve their quality of life (1989).

The last sentence, written in the passive voice, suggests that people should turn to libraries more frequently. It is indeed possible that greater use of libraries would assist people, but a missing piece of the puzzle (that is not filled in elsewhere in the report) is the knowledge, perceptiveness, and expertise of the librarian. It may be that the authors of the report employ "library" as a metonymic device. That is, it is a figure of speech intended to represent the building, the collections, the access, *and* the people. If metonymy is being used here, we should all be aware that readers of the report may not make the intended relational connection to everything, especially librarians, a library includes. When addressing the academic environment, the report does rightly note the need for incorporating learning processes that engage students and do more than present material to students. The active engagement of students is essential; moreover, the kinds of authentic or experiential learning strategies that dominate the educational literature also have a shortcoming—they do not adequately recognize that critical perception of the people's thought is also authentic (based in people's lives) and experiential.

The Committee report would provide the conceptual, albeit skeletal, foundation for the ACRL Standards that would eventually follow. Students (conceived broadly to encompass every individual who is seeking to learn) should have the following set of skills (according to the report):

- knowing when they have a need for information
- identifying information needed to address a given problem or issue
- finding needed information and evaluating the information
- organizing the information
- using the information effectively to address the problem or issue at hand (1989).

These skills, the report asserts, would enhance critical thinking and prepare people for lifelong learning. This is a quite frequently stated claim, but there is not a great deal of evidence that either critical thinking or lifelong learning can be enhanced by the skills. Regarding schools, the committee urges that information literacy be central to the workings of every school. This is a sweeping recommendation—one that should include explicit rationales *why* information literacy should be central. The importance of the rationale rests at least in the need to communicate clearly and forcefully to teachers, principals, and others. Acceptance by teachers, colleagues, and administrators is essential to success. The centrality of the above set of skills should be demonstrable and should be able to withstand challenges that put, say, reading, writing, and understanding arithmetic operations at the center. The report reads,

> The school would be interactive, because students, pursuing questions of personal interest, would be interacting with other students, with teachers, with a vast array of information resources, and the community at large to a far greater degree than they presently do today. One would expect to find every student engaged in at least one open-ended, long-term quest for an answer to a serious social, scientific, aesthetic, or politi-

cal problem. Students' quests would involve not only
searching print, electronic, and video data, but also
interviewing people inside and outside of school. As
a result, learning would be more self-initiated (1989).

Again, there is a missing rationale; a great deal appears to be taken
for granted, including the contribution to learning of students' personal
interests. The recommendation is long on form, but short on explication
of the objectives that would lead to the specifics. This is not to say that
there cannot be reasons for some specifics, but those reasons should
precede them.

A progress report on the Committee's recommendations was is-
sued in 1998, nine years after the Committee's final report. Some of
the original recommendations called for procedural action, such as
the formation of a group charged with promoting information literacy.
The National Forum on Information Literacy (http://www.infolit.org)
was established. The Forum is still active; in 2006 it co-sponsored the
Information Literacy Summit. Another call for procedural action in the
1989 report was the recommendation to work with higher education
entities to foster information literacy in programming and institutional
assessment. To reiterate some preceding points, the procedural endeavors depend on substantive messages for their success. For example,
communicating with other educational entities requires clarity and a
persuasive message. What would convince school and academic administrators to accept that information literacy deserves a place in every
curriculum? What will students gain from instructional programs?
Are librarians committed to the programs and to student learning?
Beyond the procedural elements, there remained work to be done, according to the progress report. The recommendation to enhance the
organization of, and access to, information needed attention, especially
in matters other than the technological. The fifth recommendation—to
imbue teacher education with information literacy awareness—was
deemed to have made no progress. That recommendation could be
the most far-reaching of all. It necessitates substantive transmission
and understanding, not only of the rationale for information literacy,
but curricular strategies aimed at developing instruction offered by
librarians at early stages of students' programs. Success in such an
initiative could have the potential to enhance the learning potential

of students at all levels. The recommendation has merit; the difficulty is in convincing many people of the value—actually the necessity—of libraries' instructional programs.

The ACRL Standards

The Presidential Committee's work signaled a noble effort informed by the best intentions. Unfortunately, it served to reify the particular instrumental conceptions of the objectives of libraries' instructional programs. The concentration on skills and competencies omits integrated informing, cognitive growth, and learning. The flaw contains a misconceived path that was once defined as bibliographic instruction and library instruction. Information literacy includes some admission of the inadequacy of those names, but it does not replace them with a name that is sufficiently meaningful. The limitations of the name permeate the 2000 ACRL Standards and are evident in the objectives:

An information literate individual is able to:
- Determine the extent of information needed
- Access the needed information effectively and efficiently
- Evaluate information and its sources critically
- Incorporate selected information into one's knowledge base
- Use information effectively to accomplish a specific purpose
- Understand the economic, legal, and social issues surrounding the use of information, and access and use information ethically and legally (pp. 2-3).

The Standards compound the limitation by linking the objectives to information technology skills. While an understanding of what other people say and claim does rely on some information technology skills, understanding is different from skill. An analogy may help here. For today's faculty member in higher education some information technology skills are needed to prepare manuscripts and to submit them to journals. Many journals require submission via manuscript management systems that have to be manipulated. Those skills are not directly related, though, to the articulation of a question or problem, the gathering of data, the application of a methodology, or reaching conclusions as a result of analysis. The instructional initiative is likewise peripherally connected to information technology skills.

It may be ironic, but the Standards quote a passage from *Reinventing Undergraduate Education* (http://naples.cc.sunysb.edu/Pres/

boyer.nsf/), which states that higher education should engage students in "framing a significant question or set of questions, the research or creative exploration to find answers, and the communications skills to convey the results." This admonition may be taken for granted in the Standards, but framing questions is one of the most profound cognitive actions that students can take responsibility for. Learning, creativity, and success in all endeavors depend on this ability. While framing questions includes the use of information, it is not primarily a matter of retrieving and evaluating information. There is a theme that should guide all instruction programs—the tools that are used for storage and retrieval of information are means to the end of understanding what is said, shown, or otherwise presented by other people. The effectiveness of the use of these tools is only meaningful in light of the end of understanding. The Standards include students incorporating information into their knowledge bases, but the incorporation is accomplished by the students employing logic, empirical corroboration, evaluation of testimony, and critique. Moreover, adding to one's knowledge base is only one phenomenological cognitive action; the alteration of one's knowledge base (including abandoning previously held beliefs and possibly replacing them with new beliefs) may be even more important for undergraduate students.

The expression of Performance Indicators and Outcomes may be the most problematic aspect of the Standards document. For one thing, "performance" is not necessarily indicative of learning. For example, the second Performance Indicator of the first Standard states, "The information literate student identifies a variety of types and formats of potential sources of information," is a purely instrumental skill. Discovering the differences among books, journal articles, and Web sites is independent of the critical apprehension of the content of those packages. It will likely be necessary to repeat the following statement throughout this book, but it applies almost universally to the Standards, Performance Indicators, and Outcomes: they *are definitely necessary for students' learning, but they are far from sufficient.* The first Outcome attached to the above Performance Indicator is, "Knows how information is formally and informally produced, organized, and disseminated." Such understanding is undoubtedly important, but it is most likely that the intellectual and social aspects of production will be of most value to students. The phenomena of production, organization, and dissemination are very complicated and only certain elements of the phenomena (and the technical elements are not necessarily among them) are most useful for undergraduate students. The intricacies of journal editing, book prospectus selection, and pricing (for instance) probably will not help students understand what is said. The intention behind refereeing processes (quality control through review by knowledgeable readers) is an important aspect of assessment, but the specifics of any given journal's review practices are not very useful to undergraduate students. Further, dissemination is so complicated at this time that a full understanding of it would require considerable study. The Outcome, as stated, does not present an objective that can be readily assessed. Only one additional example will be presented at this time (although many more could be mentioned). The first Performance Indicator for Standard Three reads, "The information literate student summarizes the main points to be extracted from the information gathered." The Outcomes clarify that the summary occurs *after* the student reads the text, but the Performance Indicator suggests that students should be able to anticipate what the useful components of content will be. Neither the Standard, nor the Performance Indicator, nor the Outcomes state that students should be open to unanticipated thoughts and ideas as they read, view, or listen; being able to assess alternative ideas and admit error are especially vital. The openness is essential to learning.

The application of the Standards also presents some problems. To emphasize again, libraries' instruction efforts can be an integral and effective means to enable students to learn by incorporating the thoughts of others into their overall education. The Standards, though, present instrumental tactics that appear to be self-legitimating. "Self-legitimating" is the most useful brief term I can think of to communicate an intention, conscious or not, to construct an academic function that focuses mainly on language and action that are the province of the profession. A colloquial way to express the intention is that the information literacy initiatives seek to create "little librarians." For librarians, understanding the technical structure of information-carrying packages (print resources, library catalogs, databases and aggregators, or Web sites) can be an end. The understanding, though, is employed also as a means to assist people who want to use what is *in* the packages. The Standards and their application include some of the professional objectives that are internal to, even constitutive of, librarianship. The application of the Standards in instruction carries communication that the particulars are the province of the profession. The historian communicates her knowledge in the classroom as a way to help students understand, not only the past, but the meaning of the past. The librarian, however, is successful when she helps students understand that the thought of others fosters knowledge of history, chemistry, or other disciplines. The fundamental difference between what, say, the historian and the librarian do is not acknowledged fully and functionally in the Standards.

Inferring Evaluation from the Standards

A recently published collection of essays in information literacy evaluation, gathered by Teresa Neely (2006), draws directly from the Standards. The goal of ensuring that evaluation is learning-centered is necessary and laudable. A question, though, is whether the Standards provide, in themselves, the cognitive and epistemological means to guide such evaluation. The book (Neely, 2006) implicitly claims that they are: evaluation "uses the ACRL Standards as a basic framework for developing and implementing an information literacy research agenda at the individual or institutional level, with an eye toward building a body of research literature produced by practitioners and researchers that yields usable, comparable data" (p. 3). Since the Standards are largely instrumental (skills-based), the evaluation that follows directly from them can only be instrumental as well. *The skills are necessary and important, but only as means to ends.* En route to learning about concepts—and, in particular, learning to question through awareness of a foundational background in a field—students must learn *how* to do many things. By way of analogy, it is essential that students learn grammar, syntax, and other structures of language. The purpose of learning the structures is not necessarily to make the study of structure a life's work. The purpose of learning structures of language is to enable students to understand *speech*. "Speech," as used here, is a complicated idea. It refers to the use of language as a way to construct and communicate thought. In short, students need to learn how things can be said so as to learn to understand *what* is said. "Speech" is sufficiently important that it will be revisited later. Critical thinking (and this is a potentially problematic term) depends on assessing what is said.

The means of evaluation that are demonstrated in Neely's (2006) book illustrate some of the key conceptual difficulties of using the Standards for assessment. One of the Standards revolves around students' evaluation of information. One of the means that is used as an example is the following:

Paraphrasing is the process of

a. summarizing the author's ideas in your own words

b. selecting paragraphs to use in your paper

c. changing a phrase to mean something else

d. none of the above

This query tests a student's knowledge of the concept of paraphrasing (p. 74).

The example does not really test a student's knowledge of the concept, even though there is unquestionably a correct answer. Instrumentally, it is necessary that a student be able to distinguish between quoting and paraphrasing, especially in the act of attributing thoughts, terms, or other features to someone else. To reiterate, incorporating what others think and say into one's own work is an invaluable cognitive ability. What is missing, though maybe presumed, is the intellectual act of quoting *or* paraphrasing. Imbedding the words of someone else into a context that the student establishes is a sophisticated creation. The mechanics of attribution—through quoting or paraphrasing—is a device that is part of communicative action. It is not (or should not be) a mere exercise in providing evidence of having looked at secondary sources. For example, a decision to paraphrase rather than to quote may depend on the audience for the communication. When the writer or speaker can assume audience familiarity with a concept, a brief paraphrase accomplishes both attribution and conveyance of the thought. When the writer or speaker is introducing something new or unfamiliar, a direct quotation can provide a more complete attribution *and* presentation of the thought.

The act of assessment itself presents challenges for librarians, just as it does for all teachers. The possession of skills can be demonstrated by students through application of rules or procedures (or other instrumental guides). The correct responses to requests for dates of past events in a history class, the correct use of formulae in a math class, or the correct definition of technical terms in an economics class offer teachers indications of students' readiness to proceed to more complex matters.

Likewise, the identification of titles, the ability to choose among databases for information on a specific topic, or the recognition of aspects of plagiarism can indicate to librarians that students are able to move on to more substantive matters. Another example from Neely (2006) is:

> *These* [questions] *can also be used as a starting point when developing your* [students'] *own research questions and hypotheses.*

> What are the attitudes of college-level students about Christina S. Doyle's information literacy skills?

> To what extent do students tend to overestimate their information-literacy confidence levels?

> To what extent are students unable to identify the basic elements of a bibliographic citation [emphasis added] (p. 157)?

Awareness of the basic elements of a bibliographic record does not directly enable students to frame questions or hypotheses. In this instance, and in numerous others throughout Neely's book, the concern that I have can be expressed as one of defining value.

"Value" here is not used in a moral or ethical sense, but in a particular and narrow economic one ("economic" referring to usefulness and not to monetary assignment). There is a value associated with the kinds of skills described above. That value is an instrumental one; it provides those who possess the skills with the ability to *do* certain things. For students, one value of possessing the skills is the ability to perform well on examinations designed to test the skills. Earning high grades is one measure of the instrumental value, but it is a limited one. If the measure of value is limited to performance on tests, the value of possessing the skills is likewise limited. Throughout all education there is at the very least rhetorical acknowledgment that the more meaningful value of possessing the skills is the ability to prepare students to progress beyond the instrumental level. The skills, then, are valued, not for themselves, but for the learning that students can engage in and the growth of their knowledge. Value as used here denotes a more metaphysical phenomenon, something that can enable people to accomplish things that do not have utility measures. The mistake is in not recognizing the value of intellectual growth to which the skills contribute. A question that is recommended in Neely's book (2006) in the application of the Standards is:

> When conducting research in electronic databases, how often do you use the following searching techniques? [very frequently, frequently, occasionally, infrequently, never]
>
> Truncation (search using * or $ as the last letter(s) of word, e.g., child*)
>
> Boolean operator "AND" (e.g., rivers AND pollution)
>
> Boolean operator "OR" (e.g., Blacks OR African Americans)
>
> Boolean operator "NOT" (e.g. dolphins NOT football) (p. 166).

How often students use "AND" is not a measure of value at all.

The question Neely asks raises some interesting aspects of reasoning, though, that should be explored. The principles of logic that George Boole (2005 [1854]) articulated are not used merely to manipulate technical elements of a database. The employment of "AND," "OR," and "NOT" do have the effect of altering what is retrieved as a product of a search. It is the way results are altered that is the connection to reasoning. Librarians are taught (or should have been taught in their master's programs) the fundamentals of logical linking. The instruction may use the concepts of "recall" and "precision" to emphasize some of the outcomes of logical linking. If a searcher wants high recall (retrieval of as many potentially relevant items as possible), then using "OR" is one way to ensure retrieval of a broader range of items. For example, if the searcher wants to retrieve a lot of materials on the topic "intellectual freedom," then using the term along with "censorship" (connected by "OR") will lead to the inclusion of more items in the retrieved set. If that searcher wants materials on the above topic, but in a particular environment, then the terms can be linked by "AND" with, say, "schools," OR "elementary education." This is a crude example used simply to illustrate the kind of reasoning that applies to accomplish certain objectives. Effective use of the connectors "AND," "OR," and "NOT" does not rely on mere awareness that they exist; it depends on understanding the logical reasoning that is related to the question that a student has framed. If instruction does not begin with the reasoning (not limited to the functional connectors), students are less likely to comprehend how the tools can help them achieve their purposes.

At times the goal of student learning is mentioned in information literacy assessment. Bonnie Gratch Lindauer (2004) includes student learning as a component of her tripartite evaluation matrix. Examination of the particulars of Lindauer's student learning component reveals that learning is not broadly defined. Some of her (2004) examples include,

- To what extent are information literacy learning outcomes included in course outlines, program descriptions, and syllabi? Is there an indication of how they are to be assessed>
- To what extent do course outlines and syllabi include specific assignments requiring the use of library and information resources that demonstrate specific information literacy skills?
- To what extent do program completion and graduation requirements include demonstration of information literacy? (p. 124)

"Learning," then, is limited to learning about those things that comprise information literacy. Once again, information literacy is taken to be a field independent of the matter about which others speak, write, and show. Granted, Lindauer does include possible collaboration with faculty, but this assessment plan is also instrumental in that its focus is on inclusion of the library's definition of information literacy. Questions that Lindauer (2004) suggests include,

- What is the extent to which specific information literacy learning outcomes are included in course syllabi, program descriptions and syllabi?
- What types of student performance-based measures and assessment techniques are being used for course-integrated information literacy learning opportunities?

- How do students self-assess their overall information literacy, and specific information learning outcomes? (p. 128)

The questions do not ask for anything but procedural responses; neither the content of courses or other experiences nor the enhancement of students' knowledge bases are evaluated.

A recent analysis of faculty perceptions of the ACRL Standards may embody the most telling critique of the Standards to date. While the survey is somewhat limited, the results suggest that librarians need to speak with faculty (and others) about the *conceptual foundations* related to the incorporation of what others say, write, and show into students' learning. Faculty were asked to rate the importance of Outcomes that follow from the Standards on a four-point scale ("not important" to "very important"). Seven of the Outcomes rated in the ten most important to faculty are what can be called substantive (having to do with concepts that are important in various courses). These include: plagiarism; reading texts and selecting important ideas; incorporation of textual ideas; drawing conclusions based on what is found; exploring general sources to increase familiarity with a topic clear communication to a particular audience; and recognizing bias or deception (Gullikson, 2006, p. 585). Gullikson (2006) notes in particular that faculty find the language of the Standards to be problematic: "Several surveys were returned with marginal notes asking for clarification, complaining of vagueness, or just decrying the language used (one person circled every instance of the phrase "information literate" and wrote next to one, "a horrible term!") (p. 591). The difficulty that faculty have with language *may* indicate deeper conceptual problems. This conclusion of Gullikson's suggests that much more interaction with faculty is desirable.

Enter Stanley Wilder

Readers may be wondering how this chapter could have progressed this far without the mention of a particular name—Stanley Wilder. In early 2005 Wilder published an opinion piece in the *Chronicle of Higher Education* entitled, "Information Literacy Makes All the Wrong Assumptions." Many librarians have reacted to Wilder's criticisms of information literacy; first, though, the main points of his piece should be emphasized. Wilder (2005) maintains, "The idea behind information literacy is that our typical freshman is drowning in information, when in fact Google provides her with material she find good enough" (p.

B13). That claim may be simplistic, but his observation that much of information literacy is intended to cure some pathological condition is not far off. For example, reporter Andrea Foster (2007) says, "a proliferation of information is overwhelming people and that they need help to determine what is relevant" (A39). Wilder's observation is related to an implicit intention associated with literacy in general—someone who cannot read (or cannot read well) is suffering from a deficiency that should be remedied. A poor reader is deficient, but curative action can be taken; the implicit assumption underlying information literacy is very similar. The attitude immediately creates a distance between librarian and student (some distance is inevitable and desirable, but the created distance is less than productive). It places the librarian in the dual position of diagnostician and healer (or in the position of cleric bringing salvation). The positions are not only unfortunate, they miss the point.

Why do these positions miss the point? As Wilder points out, students are not likely to think of themselves as "ill." He (2005) further says, "Information literacy tells us that [the student] cannot recognize when she needs information, nor can she find, analyze, or use it" (p. B13). Let us assume that this is a correct summary of a major aspect of information literacy (and the ACRL Standards themselves suggest that it is). Is the most effective tactic to awaken the student to her or his deficiency, and then correct it? If the student is not conscious of the deficiency, a proposed remedy may be rejected (in fact, the diagnosis may be rejected). It is here that the Standards most visibly mislead librarians. Teaching a student how to recognize when there is an information need is fruitless, since everyone is always in need of information. (This claim is rooted in the semantic dilemma presented by "information;" it will be tackled later in this chapter.) The argument here does not rest on a premise—that students have nothing to learn—quite the contrary. Instead, it rests on *what* students have to learn. Wilder's (2005) suggestion is to re-conceive information literacy skills: "librarians should view [the skills] in the same way that students and faculty members do: as an important, but ultimately mechanical, means to a much more compelling end." Information literacy, and librarianship more broadly, include tacit awareness of the more compelling ends, but the screaming of the means drowns out the plaintive calls of the ends. The calls are plaintive *because* of the complexity of the ends. More recently John Buschman (2009) has examined information literacy in the context of work being done more sweepingly on the "new literacies."

The complexity of the ends deserves more attention. In response to Wilder, Ilene Rockman (2005), in a letter to the editor of the *Chronicle of Higher Education*, says, "Students do have difficulty finding, evaluating, and using information appropriately and ethically, and we have the data to prove it from multiyear, quantitative, and qualitative studies undertaken in the California State University System" (p. B17). Let us suppose, with ample cause, that students do have these difficulties. In part the response should indeed be to help people find what will be useful to them. Before that is possible, though, people have to have fairly clear notion of what they want/need to find (they need to have some clue as to what they are looking for). These notions begin with questions, not with locations. Even faculty may fall into the trap of having difficulty finding information because they are a bit like children with hammers; their favorite resource is the hammer and every question is a nail. The hammer-and-nail standpoint is affirmed by the blogger Kiwi, who says, "Our challenge is to quit worrying about outmoded teaching and assessment measures. What we really need to be teaching instead are information literacy skills allowing (nay, requiring) students to be online" (http://kairosnews.org/blog/18). "Online" is the hammer. The solution offered by Rockman and Kiwi seems to be to give people more hammers, rather than examining what are nails and what are not. To a considerable extent, the difficulties people have are cognitive ones. There are numerous challenges to finding what is useful; the potential of phenomenological cognitive action is to alter ways of thinking about question formation and proceeding onward to responses to questions. Chapter Three will be devoted to the challenge and the potential.

Other instances of missing the point are out there; a couple of additional examples will illustrate the state of affairs. Foster (2007) relates some accomplishments of an information literacy program, but stresses some instrumental points instead of substantive ones:

> To encourage students to use scholarly material, professors here at Cal State's Fullerton campus often send their students to a computer lab, where a librarian shows them how to navigate the university's online catalog of databases, scholarly books, and journals to

do research in a particular discipline. Many journal
articles can be viewed in full online, and material
that the library does not have can be borrowed from
another library with the click of a mouse, students are
told (A39).

Her account raises a couple of concerns: (1) demonstration of the
manipulation of catalogs and databases accomplishes the objective
of familiarization with scholarly material, and (2) faculty believe the
manipulative ability fosters learning objectives. Wilder observes that
librarians like to search, other people like to find. Foster's thinking
suggests Wilder may be correct. Another example of missing the point
is Rebecca Albitz's (2007) conclusion,

> This literature survey exposes a number of disconnects
> between higher education's goal of graduating infor-
> mation literate critical thinkers and how we impart
> this knowledge to students. The initial problem is one
> of definition. Whereas librarians define the skill set
> needed to become a life-long learner as information
> literacy, teaching faculty members are more likely to
> define a similar set as critical thinking skills" (p. 107).

Institutional goals are seldom presented in terms of information
literacy, but the more important misconception is the equation of
information literacy with critical thinking. Again, the distinction is
cognitive; critical thinking involves logical, empirical, and phenomenological bases (it is original). Information literacy is instrumental (it is
derivative); the retrieval of information is a means to the end of thinking
critically about what others say, write, and show. The institutional goal
is to graduate students who can think critically *about* things. In other
words, Albitz's misconception is fundamental.

A few writers express some agreement with Wilder. Peter Williams
(2006) concurs that instruction is a means rather than an end. He adds
that, "in my experience the key to success information-skills teaching is
precisely to make a connection with the research that students are about
to embark upon" (p. 20). Williams is quite critical of the orthodoxy of
information literacy, stating that proponents, "conflate [information

literacy] with lifelong learning and appropriate the rhetoric, leading to the sort of statements highlighted here and endemic throughout the literature" (p. 20). One claim that Williams makes is debatable, though. He says that information literacy is a response to the growth in accessibility associated with expansion of the Internet and the Web. He is speaking from the perspective of the United Kingdom, and instruction there may have a somewhat different history. Many instruction programs in the U.S. predate Internet access. Some of the programs have used Jean Key Gates' book, *How to Use Books and Libraries*; the first edition of the book was published in 1962. Williams' claim is important to the purpose of the present book (and is actually something of an internal inconsistency in his own piece). Accepting that instruction of the kind promoted here is imbedded in a recognition of the means-ends distinction, the technology of the day is not constitutive of the program's purpose. Reasoning and learning through critical apprehension of what others say, write, and show forms the essential aspect of the program.

Technology and Competence

The amount of attention by writers to technology and digital information is a curious thing. As is evident from the above, some of the rationale for information literacy rests on the need to enable students to become competent users of information technologies. Students today, especially those of the traditional college age (18-22), have probably grown up digital. [At this point I am limiting discussion to four-year colleges and universities. Community and junior colleges serve somewhat different populations—older than the traditional college age and likely to have come from Kindergarten-12 school systems that have inadequate resources. Also, college age individuals who do *not* attend a college or university may also have attended less well-supported schools and may be less well-prepared for the demands of higher education.] One consequence of exposure to and experience with computers, gaming, mobile phones, and other technologies is that college and university students believe themselves to be competent, even savvy, users of technology. For many purposes the students are correct; they may have Web authoring skills, some knowledge of programming and using applications, and perhaps even understanding of hardware. By extension, the students may think themselves competent at *all* uses of technology.

In the field of psychology there has developed a body of hypotheses and research that goes by the name competency theory. This work is quite sound, but it has been used very sparingly in librarianship; in fact, Melissa Gross (2005) may be the only person writing about it in our field. She has even couched the potential for use of competency theory in terms of information literacy. She begins with the premise that librarians do not consider students' self-assessment (their impressions of their own ability) with critical scrutiny. (Bonnie Gratch Lindauer (2004) speaks of self-assessment of information literacy, but takes students' evaluations at face value.) In her review of the psychology literature Gross relates that testing consistently finds students evaluating their own competency and skill higher than they actually are. The self-assessment tends to be higher than performance on tests and assignment. Gross emphasizes that being information literate is not the same as being able to use information technologies. A conflation of the two, she (2005) says, can have consequences:

> The inability of low-performing students to self-identity skill deficits in the information-literacy realm may put them more at risk of not developing these skills as the use of electronic resources proliferates and a larger proportion of the student population opts for distance education. Because technological competence is increasingly an assumed prerequisite to participation in the digital realm, information-literacy skills may be less likely to be addressed in the general curriculum (p. 161).

Two things should be noted about Gross's observation: (1) technology (as we will see) is not the most serious problem the world of education faces, and (2) ability to make effective use of technologies *is* important, but those availing themselves of distance education opportunities may be among those most lacking in the ability. The two points will require further development.

"Information Literacy" as Name
If anyone is tempted to dismiss Wilder's criticisms, she or he should review them without a vested interest in the status quo. A reasoned

review of what Wilder says does not necessarily entail accepting it all. For one thing, his solution to integrate all instruction into reading and writing is nothing more than a nascent notion. His diagnosis, however, has quite a bit to recommend it. For someone to be able to write on a topic there must be some understanding of fundamental aspects of the topic. That understanding does indeed rely on what others say, write, and show; the understanding results from a complex set of cognitive processes. Some background on the understanding is needed before going further. What kind of understanding is required of students? What depth of understanding is needed? What expressions of understanding are insisted on by teachers? When we consider lower-division undergraduate students the answers may disappoint. Some years ago, Nobel Laureate in economics, Herbert Simon (1983), used the word "satisficing" to denote achieving or acquiring that which is good enough. Markets and choice were the subjects of his notion, but he did extend it to such areas as justice as well (pp. 85, 90). Simon's concept will be further explored in a later chapter. Wilder speaks of students satisficing (though he does not use the word) when it comes to getting good enough information to perform adequately on assignments and papers. As long as students believe that they are getting good *enough* information to get good *enough* grades, a kind of balance of effort and outcome is achieved. Traditional information literacy represents an attempt to tell students that "good enough" is not good enough; that they should strive for more. This is a tough sell to the students. A different tack may be more fruitful (and that tack will be discussed later in this chapter).

Some of the strengths of Wilder's critique are enforced by the results of Gullikson's survey. The language of the Standards is imprecise at times, so much so that it is difficult to discern meaning. The meaning may be clear to librarians who work with systems and their structures, but may be less clear to students and, perhaps, faculty. Outcome d of Performance Indicator 1 of Standard Two (in itself a confusing hierarchical arrangement) states, "Selects efficient and effective approaches for accessing the information needed from the investigative method or information retrieval system." This is a difficult Outcome to assess, given the obtuseness of its language. A goal for information literacy is the integration of these Standards into course syllabi; it would be an uphill battle to convince a teacher to add the above statement. The teacher might say that such activity would take time away from the subject matter of the course. Outcome c of Performance Indicator 3 of Standard Four reads, "Incorporates principles of design and communication." Even in the context of the Standard and Performance Indicator, this Outcome has little meaning. What principles of design; what is design?

The respondent to Gullikson's survey who said that "information literacy" is a horrible term is on to something. First, the word "literacy" is problematic. The function of comprehending sentences is necessary, but it is far short of being able to follow complicated narratives or arguments, to interpret from figures of speech or irony, or to communicate complex ideas. Similarly, recognition of "author" as opposed to "title" in fields of a database or in citations is not identical to being able to understand the contents of articles, books, or Web sites sufficiently to incorporate them into one's own work or to critique them. "Literacy" at once says too much and too little. It says too much in that it suggests a specific intellectual function, whereas the ability is more generic. It says too little, as was just hinted, in that it suggests only regulated functioning, whereas the ability is more of a constitutive form of reasoning. Edward Stevens (1987) relates a similar assessment of literacy (in general) in his examination of social and political uses of literacy. If "information literacy" is in part intended to lend legitimacy to instruction programs, then it has both nominal and substantive problems. The term may not be well understood by faculty; if that is the case, will it be understood by students?

The notion of information literacy as a remedy for a pathology, described above, is all too pervasive. The notion has led to the tagging of the word "literacy" on to any number of modifiers—media literacy, political literacy, technological literacy, visual literacy, etc. (Many such modifiers of literacy are defined at the National Forum on Information Literacy Web site—http://www.infolit.org/definitions.html). The most potent, and charged, representation of the trend is "cultural literacy" as defined by E. D. Hirsch (1988). The appendix to his book is a list of names, dates, titles, and events. Awareness of the items on the list constitutes, for Hirsch, cultural literacy, and the list itself *is* the remedy. In fact, it is a reasonable and necessary objective to locate and address what might be called deficiencies (the inability to place people, times, and events within a larger context, in the case of cultural literacy). If a high school student is functionally illiterate, then the school and the teachers should take appropriate action; the action is the school's duty. Limited to such a diagnostic and remedial definition, literacy has meaning. It connotes a base of functioning, offers a way to evaluate people's ability, and suggests means to help people acquire the base of functioning.

Hirsch's book and the ACRL Standards have something in common. Both begin with the assumption that something is broken, and proceed with a prescription to fix it. The "something" is not entirely delineated though, since culture and information, for example, are not only broad concepts, but are contested as well. I use "prescription" on purpose here; both Hirsch and ACRL prescribe the fix. Follow their instructions and the problem will be repaired. Whether prescription is deliberate or not for the creators, the use of lists presents prescribed paths—beginnings and ends. The lists may not be ordinal or hierarchical, but they almost cannot be presented any other way. For instance, should ACRL Standard One be completed before moving on to Standard Two? Should someone be aware of the date 1066 before becoming aware of the date 1492? As Webber and Johnston (2000) observe, the list approach "fragments the field of knowledge and reflects a 'surface learning' approach (with a short-term focus on the task in hand) rather than a 'deep learning' one (in which the students are encouraged to reflect on and contextualise what they are learning, in a manner that enables them to use the knowledge or skill outside the task in hand)" (p. 384). Although he does not develop the point, Edward Owusu-Ansah (2003) says that literacy in general tends to be behaviorist (p. 221). The operational assumption that lists are indeed hierarchical does include an implication that students should be conditioned.

Changing Behavior

Owusu-Ansah's comment on the behaviorist bent of literacy could apply to much of education. Constructivism has already been discussed, but it is very common for teachers at all levels to establish rubrics of performance and to insist that students' actions be in concert with the rubrics. In many dictionaries the first definition of "rubric" has it being an authoritative rule, sometimes in general, but frequently in the conduct of a liturgical service. The definition underscores a challenge for educators. One way students learn is through the application of rules. Rules of grammar, for instance, enhance the clarity of spoken and written communication. What this boils down to is that rubrics are certainly not bad things. Heidi Goodrich Andrade (2000) presents an illustration of a rubric she uses in teaching writing to seventh and eighth graders. Students at that age are novices at expository and persuasive writing; the rubric provides guidance for them. (Note: Andrade's rubric is intended for instructional, and not merely for scoring, purposes.) In another work Andrade (2005) stresses that using rubrics solely for scoring can lead to students mindlessly following rules (p. 20). It is that scoring or grading function that can impress upon students the primacy of the rules to the detriment of learning.

The behaviorism in education can be referred to as deliberate, but less than conscious. There is deliberate decision making that is imbedded in teaching and assessment, but teachers, if asked, would be likely to deny that behaviorism informs their decisions at all. The Standards are examples of the phenomenon. A tension follows the introduction of the decisions and some of what underlies them. Imagine someone saying to you that what you are doing follows behaviorist psychology. It is quite possible that you would deny what the person is accusing you of; you believe you are not following behaviorist psychology. Your denial may be based on your recognition of behaviorism's psychological and philosophical shortcomings. You may also feel some unease; you may even ask yourself if this person could possibly be correct. The reactions would be understandable; if something is not conscious then you *cannot* be aware of it. Going further, if there is a behaviorist element to your decision, you probably did not insert it intentionally. Once you were told that someone perceives a behaviorist element, what do you do? The responsible action would be to examine your actions in light of what has been said to you. Just because the person said that behaviorism is influencing what you are doing does not make it so. On the other hand, critical self-examination according to phenomenological cognitive action is required.

If it is said that information literacy does in fact have a behaviorist element, the burden is on the speaker to provide evidence for that conclusion. For the time being, the Standards will be the source of evidence; in a later chapter, courses and their content will be examined and the matter will arise again. The first order of business is to define behaviorism, and B. F. Skinner is a legitimate starting place. He (1953) states that a behaviorist approach is concerned, first, with the causes of human behavior—"By discovering and analyzing these causes we can predict behavior; to the extent that we can manipulate them, we can control behavior" (p. 23). Turning, then, to the challenge of manipulation he writes, "operant reinforcement... improves the efficiency of behavior and maintains behavior in strength long after acquisition or efficiency has ceased to be of interest" (p. 66). That particular reinforcement presents a difficulty for all educators; an objective is to motivate people to learn, but institutional regulation prescribes that grades must be given. A problem is to provide intellectual motivation while avoiding any conditioning that may accompany grades. This is a serious tension; the very structure of higher education and its requirements of assigning grades heighten the tension. The tension is further exacerbated by some attractiveness of behaviorism that seems to mitigate the control element (or at least to hide it). Skinner (1953) addresses education specifically: "In an American school if you ask for the salt in good French, you get an A. In France you get the salt. The difference reveals the nature of educational control. Education is the establishing of behavior which will be of advantage to the individual and to others at some future time" (p. 402). We will have to realize that, even admitting the usefulness that Skinner introduces, a vital component is absent from behaviorism—understanding. (The word "understanding" is written of by Skinner, but only as an example of successful conditioning.)

Skinner's behaviorism is strong and reductive. It is the kind of thinking that has given behaviorism the bad reputation it has. As is stated above, rubrics (or rules) can assist students in mastering some elements of particular intellectual tasks. When the rubrics are presented in such a way that students think critically about the necessity for and uses of the rules, the students gain an understanding of *why* the rules exist. Subject-verb agreement is one simple rule that can help students understand that the agreement ensures clarity. Further, the rule insists that the student—as writer and speaker—comprehends the meaning that she or he wants to convey. Behaviorism as a tool for manipulation has little or nothing to do with understanding; the purpose is control of the actions of others (the antithesis of phenomenology). The book and film, *The Manchurian Candidate*, is a stark example of control. Skinner's thought has been connected to the positivist program of the twentieth century (only observation and empirical analysis can lead to knowledge) and to inductivism (Skinner had no use at all for theories and hypotheses). His flawed thinking may be most evident in his ideas on language. Laurence Smith (1986) recounts that, "For Skinner, what is traditionally spoken of as the 'meaning' or 'reference' of a term was to be found only in its actual use. In this radically naturalized account of meaning, there could be no relation of correspondence between a term and its referent, much less between a mentalistic 'idea' and some object that it stands for" (p. 285). Because of the potential attractiveness of Skinner's behaviorism (educators must be wary of the temptation of empiricism without conceptualization, as well as uninformed induction), his work, while not necessarily cited, may influence course content and pedagogical action, in libraries' instructional programs and beyond.

What Is Information?

Earlier on I mentioned that the Standards suggest some behaviorist tendencies. This claim is consistent with all of the foregoing criticisms of the Standards and of "information literacy." The third Performance Indicator of Standard One is, "The information literate student considers the costs and benefits of acquiring the needed information." This Indicator places becoming informed, or becoming more knowledgeable, about something within an economic (this time with definable costs and benefits) transaction. It can have a value (or price) placed on it, and that value can be compared with the value of the time it takes to learn something. First, this requires the student to know these values in advance of the action; this assumes many of the worst qualities of what is called "rational choice theory." Rational choice theory, developed by economists as an aid in understanding the decisions consumers make in a variety of markets, makes a number of unfounded assumptions about rationality and human action. Donald Green and Ian Shapiro (1994) write that,

> rational choice theorists generally agree on an instrumental conception of individual rationality, by reference to which people are thought to maximize their expected utilities in formally predictable ways. In empirical applications, the further assumption is generally shared that rationality is homogeneous across the individuals under study (p. 17).

An important lesson for instructional programs is not to fall into rational choice theory's trap of being method-driven instead of problem-driven. Also, rational choice theory, and some aspects of the Standards, requires *a priori* awareness of costs, outcomes, and other elements of the future. What happens when we do not have this *a priori* awareness?

More importantly, the Indicator reduces learning assisted by assessing what others say, write, and show to a transaction. It has no discernible value in itself, and has only some instrumental value that can be measured. This may perhaps summarize the shortcomings of the Standards and the employment of the unfortunate name, "information literacy." The shortcomings are demonstrated in other excerpts from the Standards, such as Standard Two: "The information literate student accesses needed information effectively and efficiently." This Standard falls prey to presuming that students begin the action of finding information with a clearly defined "need." The presumption is reinforced by Outcome a under Performance Indicator 4 of Standard Three: "Determines whether information satisfies the research or other information need." If an objective of instruction is to identify information needs and then to satisfy them, information literacy is an economic action governed by predictable and manipulable behaviors. Information literacy is an exercise of control.

As problematic as "literacy" is, "information" is at least as challenging. The first problem we face is one of meaning—how can information be defined? The answer is not satisfying; information is taken to mean many, something contradictory, things. More than half a century ago Claude Shannon published his influential work on information theory. Shannon was an engineer working for Bell Labs; his aim was to find ways to ensure the fidelity of transmissions over telephone and telegraph lines. Some recent advertisements for cell phone networks demonstrate that dropped calls can cause misunderstanding by interrupting messages. These ads illustrate the problem that Shannon was trying to solve. As part of his work he constructed a mathematical theory of communication to assist with the definition and solution of the problem. At the heart of his theory is his borrowing the concept of entropy from Isaac Newton. Increases in the amount of "information" lead to disorder (in the statistical sense), further leading to the difficulty of transmitting meaningful messages. Information, for Shannon, is that measure of disorder, or entropy. The more information that exists, using Shannon's terminology, the more choices one has for selecting possible meanings of a message. Ernest Hemingway's prose has a low entropy value; his sentences tend to be short and simple and he uses words in straightforward and realistic ways. William Faulkner, on the other hand, has a complex prose style; sentences can run on for pages. A natural language, like English, has rules (once again there is the need for some rules) of grammar, syntax, morphology, and so on. It also has an agreed-upon vocabulary (that, admittedly, does not include single definitions for every word). The structures of languages enable understandable communication, at least to a substantial degree. Shannon's conception is not necessarily directly related to "information literacy," but it is used widely to illustrate the potential manipulability of information. The manipulability is indeed a component of many conceptions of information literacy.

The operational, but unstated, definition of "information" in information literacy is perhaps the most problematic of all. Information, as it tends to be used, is a physical (in the sense that it exists) entity that has some economic value, but carries no meaning. This is an extreme statement, but I do believe it can be defended. As is evident in the Standards, information can be transmitted, received, and used in some way. It has some relation to unspecified needs; it has some value. The lack of specification is one of the reasons I maintain that this conception of information does not include the sharing of meaning. The need is reduced to a physical expression, akin to hunger; the need is satisfied by access to something. The point of information literacy is to enable students to gain access to something when they have the need. Instruction, then, is diagnostic and remedial. The remedy is to get students to the point where they can satisfy their own needs. Information, in this usage, signifies nothing. This is not a Shakespearean trope; it is a semiotic failing. Semiotics was introduced very briefly at the end of Chapter One. While semiotic study can be complicated, some fundamentals are quite straightforward. For a sign system to work there must be at least two components—a signifier (the part of the sign that is intended to refer to something) and a signified (the part that is intended to be the referent or object of the sign). A third component has been introduced by some writers (and this component is necessary for the complete functioning of the system). An interpretant—the sense that is made of the sign structure—is needed because the act of interpretation is not simply a response to a stimulus. Think of figures of speech, such as metaphors or similes. They have literal meanings, but speakers and writers do not employ them for their literal possibility. An act of interpretation is required for a hearer or reader to have full appreciation of the metaphor.

Language itself presents everyone with some difficulties, though. It is possible for one signifier to have more than one signified. "Saturn" as signifier may refer to an automobile or a planet (among other things). Context will usually make clear which signified relates to an interpretant. There are times when context is not helpful. At these times the possibilities for various, even competing, interpretants are numerous. The root of the problem is that there are various, even competing, signifieds. "Information" presents just such a problem. It now has many theoretical, operational, and colloquial meanings, but as a signifier it is still used as if it has a single signified. The Standards, for example, treat it in a tautological way; information literacy is the ability to recognize the need for information and the ability to locate information. But what is information? How does one recognize a need for information? To reiterate, in usages that include the Standards, information is some form of tradable commodity. Even when theorists attempt to clarify matters, questions remain. Robert Losee (1997) writes, "Information is produced by all processes and it is the values of characteristics in the processes' output that are information." Information, then, is everything (or everything that has any value in the narrow economic sense). The confusion may constitute an interesting philosophical challenge, but it renders a program ostensibly based on some normative signified almost impossible.

"Information" is also intended to have meaning when people speak of the information society. It may be hoped that students will be able to function more capably in the information society. Tacking "society" on to the word does not help much, though. Information society is variously taken to mean contests between liberation and oppression, wealth and poverty, advance and regress. Frequently the term is used to represent the expansion of capital markets; at other times it is taken to represent freedom from controlling forces. Frank Webster (1995) reviews uses of the word and recognizes that there is usually a connection to technology, which tends to coincide with markets, commerce, and capitalism. The information society is more productive because more output can be generated by less labor. He notes that some commentators say information is an independent thing, not reliant at all on human perception for its existence. Information literacy discourse does not explicitly go so far, but the independence of information lurks in the Standards and elsewhere. Another point where information society and information literacy intersect is the uncritical acceptance that there has been a technological revolution from which an information age has sprung. There have indeed been some transforming developments, but the nature of the revolution (if a revolution has occurred) is frequently left unexamined.

There is a name for the kind of difficulty that "information" poses. Since it is not possible to arrive at an interpretant, "information" can be called an empty signifier, or a floating signifier. I may speak of information literacy to you, and I may have a very specific signified in mind. If I do not make that signified clear through additional sign structures, you may insert your own interpretant. Much of the discourse on information literacy side-steps the problem altogether; "information" is left as an empty signifier. Until this problem is acknowledged and addressed directly, librarianship will continue to engage in practices that lack direction. A tacit assumption appears to govern use of "information" in information literacy—information is a physical thing that, by virtue of its properties, is knowable and transmissible in meaningful ways. In other words, there is an assumption that we have facts about information, and that we can design instructional programs based on those facts. If the physical meaning is not intended, then there is the need for explication. As an empty signifier, though, information comes from everything, so the design of a program constantly loses direction. An explicit recognition could replace the tacit assumption. Sign systems are not naturally occurring things; they are intentionally constructed. There are social, political, and historical elements of sign systems and their use. With empty signifiers intentionality is either lost or perverted. It can be perverted for ideological purposes (that is, purposes of domination of control); as such a signifier can be purposely left empty. In the instance of information literacy, intentionality is lost; the coiners of the term probably meant something by it, but that meaning has been replaced by a circulating mélange of possible meanings.

Is There a Solution?

I would not be writing this book if I did not believe that librarianship can design meaningful instruction programs. The previously used names for instruction—library instruction and bibliographic instruction—were clear signifiers. People recognized, though, that the signifieds that emerge from these signifiers were inadequate. It is not merely the library that is important to student learning. The recognition was correct, but the alternative presented was not an improvement. [If librarianship can transcend "literacy," the entire notion of good enough vs. not good enough disappears. The focus turns to learning and instilling in students a different way to think about learning.] The expression of purpose in the Standards makes it look like the name "information literacy" came first and then its definition followed. That may not have been the case, but the emptiness of the signifier results nonetheless. This chapter has been very critical of the discourse and thinking that has led to the signifier "information literacy." It is time to return to the most fundamental examination of need and ways to address the need.

Barbara D'Angelo and Barry Maid (2004) observe that, "the ability of librarians to effect curricular change remains limited" (p. 212). Combine this observation with some of the results of Gullikson's survey and reasons for the difficulty suggest themselves. First, is curricular change a goal? If it is, then what kinds of changes are needed; what is not occurring that should occur? What are the intended outcomes of the change? These are some of the questions for which there are inadequate answers in our professional discourse. The goal is not to insinuate librarians into teaching positions. That may well occur (it probably should occur), but it is not the starting place. Before there is an impetus for change there should be a reason for change. That reason is imbedded in the entirety of higher education's purpose. Students are not gaining sufficient understanding of the social, humanistic, and scientific essences of humankind. The lacunae manifest themselves in many ways. Students have little awareness of the historical background that helps us understand where we are now and how we got here. Students are ignorant of basic biological, chemical, and physical facts; this limits their ability to understand aspects of the world and human life in the world. Students are not able to examine social structures that affect politics, economics, law, and many other forms of human action. One cause for the problem is that students are not sufficiently educated with regard to the critical evaluation of what others say, write, and show, and to incorporate that evaluation into their own education. In short, there is insufficient apparatus for students to build bases of knowledge.

The aforementioned problems certainly do not begin with higher education. Schooling at all levels needs to address the problems directly. But when students attend colleges and universities the problems that began earlier continue. Academic libraries are much more than repositories for physical materials, and herein is the first step on a path to a solution for the instructional challenge. Libraries and education share something in common; they do not depend on information, they depend on communication. The difference is profound. Information, as an empty signifier, contributes little or nothing to learning and knowledge. Communication, as action, signifies both speaking and hearing, both writing and reading. Most of the work that constitutes librarianship consists of communicating. Catalogs communicate ways to access what others have written, and also ways to group writings on similar subjects. Reference services are intended to communicate the nature of questioning and the ways to answer questions. Design of, and work with, technical systems are ways to enable communication between those who want to find useful speech and the speech itself. Teaching and learning are exercises of communication, not simply as the imparting of facts, but as dialogues that foster understanding. Moreover, communication, when it works most effectively, is phenomenological; it incorporates self and other along with the aim of intentionality. Replacing "information" with "communication" can help us lose the notion of transactions and objectified things.

The first chapter brought up the need for a dialectical approach to instructional programs. Information literacy has no room for dialectic, though. In presenting lists, the official discourse on information literacy says that there is one set of objectives and one set of outcomes. In simple terms, there is no possibility for theses and antitheses. A more fully realized dialectical approach can emphasize critique—the exploration of conflict, even contradiction, and examination of logical, social, political, and economic sources of conflict. The presumption that there are needs, and that the needs can be met by instrumental processes, transmits to students the idea that learning can be reduced to skills and competencies in the narrow sense of developing particular behaviors. A dialectical approach places a greater intellectual responsibility on the students. In fact, libraries' instructional programs may be a good place to introduce dialectic.

Lower-division undergraduate students may not be accustomed to having substantial responsibility for their learning, so introducing them to critique in the context of the foundational place of what others say, write, and show could attune them to a dialectical attitude. The context is a means to insinuate a phenomenological aspect into learning.

The purpose of an instructional program is not to remedy a deficiency or to heal an illness. Its purpose may be most effectively realized as attunement to the place of communication in learning. The process of searching a catalog or a database is one of communication; it is dialogic. The books and the articles that are retrieved through the search process are speech acts; they are intentional communications. Understanding of the speech act nature of these forms of communication is essential to cognitive action. Students can think about an article as a speech act, as someone's communication with him or her. That recognition can open the possibility of dialogue. The actions of reading and listening are not passive; they are not the absorption of data. A reader questions, wonders why, places what is written into a familiar context. The context itself is created dialogically through a lifetime of listening, reading, questioning, and wondering. If schooling prior to attendance at a college or university has not invited dialogic participation, then the college or university must initiate it. It is in this regard that learning can be constructed.

Placing communication at the center of attention leads to awareness of *what* is communicated. In academic settings, the kind of communication, and the content of communication can be fairly narrowly defined. The lectures and discussions in the classrooms, the course readings and texts, out-of-class conversations, and technologically mediated discourse focus on the subject matter of courses of study. A course in nineteenth-century American fiction limits communication (overwhelmingly) to that topic. Discussion in the course may include the lives of authors, the social and political times in which works were written, conventions and strictures imposed by society, and so on. The purpose of the communication may be to enhance students' understanding of nature of fiction writing at a particular time and place, to foster aesthetic appreciation for works of literature, to demonstrate that literary art is not separate from the rest of life, and other things. Within the course the teacher might establish the purposes and set guidelines for the communicative action of the class. If it is an advanced course students may be required to read criticism and theory related to the course content. In order for that communication to be successful the teacher and the students must understand why the critics and theorists are writing, to whom they write, and how to read them. Understanding of the communicative action that is essential in higher education is not a by-product of education, *it is constitutive of education.*

I emphasize that point, but it is too frequently unacknowledged. The best teachers may comprehend the importance of the communicative action, and they may use it to great effect in helping students learn. All teachers can be more effective if they have a full appreciation for the essential character of communication. The teachers are presumed to know the subject matter; the educational impetus is for the teachers to share with students by communicating with them, so that the students' knowledge grows. The contribution that librarians can make is to place communication at the center of the process. Librarians are likely to have the clearest understanding of the flow of communication, including the reasons why it flows as it does. I would not claim that teaching faculty have so clear an understanding. The understanding is not entirely independent of technology or means of transmission, but it is of a higher order than the technical manipulation of files. This chapter has been very critical of "information literacy" as name and as idea; I propose that we replace the statement of purpose attached to defining information literacy with a statement that is aimed directly at the central function of higher education.

> Libraries' instructional programs are invaluable to facilitating learning, knowledge growth, and communication. Librarians can enable understanding of the nature and purposes of communication, help students engage in dialogue with what others say, write, and show, and foster, through phenomenological cognitive action, student learning.

With the critique established, we can proceed to examination of the content of instructional programs in the form of courses offered by libraries and librarians.

KEY POINTS IN CHAPTER TWO:

➤   Over the last couple of decades there have been some efforts to define information literacy in ways that transcend older concepts, such as bibliographic instruction; the definitions themselves have contributed to the development of the ACRL Standards

➤   Evaluation features prominently in the Standards and in much of the discourse on information literacy; the challenge still remains to conceive of evaluation more substantively and less instrumentally

➤   There have been some individuals who have argued against the most frequently expressed ideas about information literacy; the counter-arguments tend to fall back on the mechanics of searching, retrieving, and other processes

➤   Competence may be an attractive objective for instruction programs and session; it is a necessary objective, but it is not sufficient to achieve understanding of what is written, said, and shown

➤   The understanding that teachers want students to obtain depends on semantically and semiotically clear conceptions of the purposes of instruction (the conceptions must be meaningful and must signify precisely what is to be learned)

CHAPTER THREE

◆

In the Classroom

In their introduction to their substantial work on information literacy, Esther Grassian and Joan Kaplowitz (2001) write, "Information literacy has reached a new stage of importance in the professional consciousness of librarians" (p. xxvii). They then use the definition that has been mentioned here and that is included in the ACRL Standards. Based on their use of the definition and their opening statement, it seems to me that they are partially correct, but there are some troubling difficulties. The partial correctness lies in the recognition of the importance of instruction. Their incorrectness is grounded in the definition. The difficulties are most evident in their chapter on learning theory. A few theories are presented more or less uncritically and superficially, so that behaviorism is on a par with other approaches. Their review of other theories reifies notions that are popularly phased as teachers being "guides on the side," rather than "sages on the stage." Students who are active in educational processes can enhance their learning and discovery, but undergraduate students are still developing cognitively, especially in the realm of metacognition. Because of the developmental limitations, students should be taught how to think about what people say, write, and show. Numerous works suggest that students have a tendency to accept what they come across, so the metacognitive processes of awareness of one's own thought are necessary for substantive (and not simply surface) evaluation. Particulars of metacognition will be addressed in the next chapter, but examination of instructional programs cannot ignore the necessary cognitive processes.

It is in practice where the ideas of such things as official documents (the Standards included) are put into action. The framework of phenomenological cognitive action applies also to course design, course content, and pedagogy. Librarians as instructors are engaged in particular kinds of cognition as they conceive of the education of undergraduate students. The cognitive challenges are complex, as we will see, and include imagining the states that students are in, relative to librarians' own states. This is a challenge that all teachers, at all levels, face. You may know something; can you put yourself in the position of someone who does *not* know that thing? The challenge is heightened with the realization that teachers have to recognize that students may not know *how* to think about some things. These challenges may actually be the soundest bases in favor of libraries' instructional programs as comprising required courses in colleges and universities. Higher education faculty and administrators are coming to accept that little can be taken for granted with regard to the cognitive and knowledge states of beginning students. When it comes to enhancing the potential for student success (defined in terms of leaning, not just grades), foundational experiences that include libraries' instructional programs are invaluable, at least in principle. In addition to what students bring to the classroom, teachers' presentation (how they introduce students to ideas and thoughts) is extremely important. Many campuses have courses, frequently freshman-level courses, that have the word "rhetoric" in the title. The existence of the courses does not mean that libraries' instructional programs can ignore rhetoric. Its importance will be built upon in this chapter. Before the ideal contribution of libraries' instructional programs is valorized, though, some attention to the actual content of programs is necessary.

Instructional Content
The examination by Paul Hrycaj (2006) of for-credit courses offered by libraries was mentioned very briefly earlier. His analysis of the course content provides an indication of what is covered in the courses and, as he says, can be used to discuss what *should* be covered. Some of his findings should be reiterated here. Hrycaj (2006) did note that the 100 courses he examined included frequent treatment related to ACRL Standard Two (effective and efficient access to needed information). He also found that there was very little representation of Standard Four (effective use of information to accomplish specific purposes) (p. 529). The findings tend to corroborate my claim that instrumental and procedural elements of information use outweigh substantive and critical elements. If enhancement of students' critical thinking is an objective of courses, and if the Standards inform course content, then one would

expect to see more attention to Standard Four. In fact, it is Standard Four that offers the most substantive guidance for the design and assessment of instruction. Hrycaj (2006) also found that Standard Three (evaluation and critical incorporation of information) is represented by less than half the frequency of Standard Two, further indicating focus on mechanics of access and searching.

Hrycaj (2006) also tracked particular topics that syllabi included. He identified seven topics that were included in at least three-fourths of the syllabi; they were: periodicals databases; Web searching; online catalog; Web site evaluation; writing citations; monograph evaluation; research strategy (p. 528). The topics tend to be procedural and deal with the instrumental actions of searching and retrieving. These topics are necessary and should be included in courses, but, again, they are means to ends. "Research topics" is a component of just over half of the syllabi, so a question that can be asked relates to the context in which access and searching is introduced. Hrycaj (2006) also indicated that some seemingly important topics are infrequently covered: concept of information; writing a research paper; how information is produced (p. 528). Even with topics on evaluation there appear to be limitations: "Such evaluation of sources can focus on evaluative criteria such as currency, authority, documentation of sources, and bias, which can be determined without necessarily delving into the actual content of the sources" (Hrycaj, 2006, p. 530). Hrycaj recognized the extent to which his analysis has boundaries, but his work should be read very closely. As he concludes,

> In summary, this study of online syllabi gives qualified support to the author's hypothesis that matters of information access… are the dominant subject matter of credit-bearing college and university library skills courses…. But the other parts of Standard Three, dealing with critical thinking and information synthesis, did not appear to have much representation in the syllabi (p. 533).

Communication in the Classroom
One of the things that all academic librarians should be interested in is the kind of communication that takes place in instructional programs.

A thorough understanding of communication practices would require attendance in classes; examination of syllabi, tutorials, and other readily accessible materials can provide some limited insight into communication. Communication is, of course, integral to any teaching-learning experience. Particulars can vary, but lecture, Socratic questioning, student-created work, and all other pedagogical types rely entirely on effective communication. This necessity is brought home in the last chapter in the context of "information literacy" as name. The names of courses can be the first things that students see, so metaphorical or otherwise rhetorical names may amuse faculty but may not be meaningful to students.

At some colleges and universities the form and elements of course syllabi may be prescribed. The prescription may not be a burden, though, if the possibility exists to include as much detail as needed. Beyond any institutional requirements there is the matter of syllabus construction. What information about the course should it include? How much detail is needed? What *kinds* of detail are necessary? A challenge throughout higher education is the inadequate preparation of teachers is the design of syllabi. Many teachers tend to adopt the models they have been exposed to. One result of the inattention to syllabi is that little thought is given by teachers to what a syllabus communicates to students. Syllabus content, therefore, can all too often be minimal and fulfills only administrative requirements. Most importantly, too few teachers think of a syllabus as a thorough plan for the course—something not only for students to use as a guide, but as an intentional strategy for teaching and learning. The shortcomings that may plague many of the course offerings need not afflict libraries' instructional programs.

The review of some for-credit course offerings in libraries reveals that some of the syllabi could actually be used as models on their campuses. In such cases, the communicative potential of a syllabus is realized. One example of an effective syllabus is that of Lakeland Community College in Illinois (http://webclass.lakeland.cc.il.us/info_lit/syllabus.html). (The URL presented here might not be functional by the time this is read; Lakeland may still employ the syllabus, though.) The designers of the syllabus created a very rich environment online; students are not overloaded with information all at once. Links imbedded within the main structure of the syllabus lead students to detail on the specific items. For example, in week three of the course there is a link to assist students with the topic of searching the online catalog. Moreover, the course introduces the students to the more generic nature of online catalogs, regardless of the specific library used. From the course site:

What are some features of online catalogs?

- Since you can access the catalog through the internet, you don't have to be in the library to use it. You can search your local library's collection from your own home to find out if they have what you're looking for, before you make the trip there. You could even search the collection of a library halfway across the world.
- Online catalogs allow you to search through thousands of records in seconds, and you can manipulate your search in many different ways. You can combine different search terms or restrict your search to only a certain format, such as DVDs, for example.
- Online catalogs don't just tell you what the library owns, but will also tell you whether the item is available right now or checked out.
- Many online catalogs are system-wide, which means you can search the collections of dozens of libraries all at the same time.
- Many online catalogs allow you to request items, renew items, and check your account from the convenience of your computer.
- Librarians love their online catalogs so much they often give them names. Some examples of catalog names are Millinet, WorldCat, Mirlyn, and ORCA. These are often abbreviations or acronyms.

This syllabus offers considerable detail and is presented in a manner that is amenable to focus on the course topics; in short, it is informative.

Since many of the syllabi are readily accessible via the Web, there is the possibility for a kind of tacit collaboration—collegial sharing of effective practices is simplified. The accessibility also makes possible some examination of syllabi. A few are perused here; this is a convenience sample of a dozen selected only for their completeness and used here solely as illustrations of some that are employed now. The institutions will not be named here. Six of the twelve syllabi examined make explicit reference to the ALA definition of information literacy and to the ACRL Standards. These references are not merely informational; the definition and the Standards are used to establish the framework for the courses and to shape the course content. That is, these syllabi follow the Standards to a considerable extent. As Hrycaj (2006) observes, evaluation receives less attention than do searching, retrieving, and packages of content (not merely in the six, but in all twelve). The mechanics of searching the library's catalog, databases, and the Web occupies a substantial amount of course time. Assignments and examples tend to focus on searchable fields, protocols, and Boolean connectors. One library's syllabus states that, "Students will develop effective strategies for using information technologies when seeking knowledge." Another explicitly mentions scholarly communication patterns (while this topic did not arise in other syllabi among the twelve, it does occur in the syllabi of a number of courses and instructional sessions, particularly in single sessions where librarians speak to graduate and upper-division undergraduate courses). That syllabus also addresses the social contexts in which information is produced, disseminated, and used.

One of the twelve syllabi claims that the course is intended to help students succeed academically. This goal may be implicit in all courses, but it is an essential element to mention to students; there is a pragmatic benefit to the courses for students. Only a couple of these course syllabi include ethics, especially plagiarism. Ethics is, of course, the body of one of the ACRL Standards, and is vital, especially for beginning students, to become aware of. The practices of acknowledgement and citation are integral to intellectual integrity, but may not have been introduced to students prior to their enrollment in college. A library's course can ensure that students are aware of the ethical obligation of honesty, as well as the procedures for demonstrating honest practice. On a related note, one syllabus includes the statement that, "Information is a commodity." The syllabus does not add a rationale for the statement, although it may be a component of the course content. The statement, while not demonstrably incorrect (packages and access are bought and sold), imbues a particular conception of information into the course. Information is much more than a commodity; it can be a matter of public discourse and debate, it can define regulations and obligations within society, and it can be an element of education. The statement emphasizes the instrumental nature that some courses may have in that it stresses the "thing" while deemphasizing communicable ideas and thoughts. This brief review of a few syllabi is intended only to provide a bit more evidence for the received view of instruction (the professional documents and discourse that places instruction within a limited territory); the fundamentals of learning through active engagement of ideas are underrepresented.

The Syllabus

One way to avoid a shortcoming of syllabus design is to investigate the language of the syllabus itself as part of the class. This is very seldom done in higher education at large; instructors present the syllabus to the students and may occasionally ask if the students have any questions. The request for questions offers the illusion of dialogue, but communication is usually not very effective. If a student wonders why certain topics are covered, or how topics connect to the course objectives, that student may not vocalize the questions. The questions are legitimate; they can indicate some lack of clarity in the syllabus. The questions could be perceived—by both student and teacher—as unnecessary. In the worst cases students could complete the course, but never be confident about its purpose, its organization, its flow, etc. Also in the worst cases, the instructors are oblivious to the students' confusion and they firmly believe that they have been clear. When a syllabus is unclear, one of two things is likely to follow: (1) time in class (at times well into the course) is spent trying to correct misunderstanding and fostering a common meaning, or (2) nothing more is said about the course's purpose, objectives, connections among topics, or other elements of the course's essential character. In the first instance there is at least the possibility for clarity and continuity. In the second instance those goals may be irrevocably compromised.

Libraries' instructional programs, and especially the teachers, must also take care to avoid a trap that many academics fall into. The classroom—virtual or physical—is a locus of power. The teacher (in just about all courses) determines the structure, content, and flow of the course. The teacher selects the readings and other supporting materials. The teacher controls speech. The power that rests with the teacher is itself neither good nor bad; someone has to set the direction for the course and be responsible for the particulars. Some teachers, probably as far back as the first teachers, have abused the power by skewing content, injecting bias, and stifling students' speech. Many more teachers have sought to foster freedom while guiding students along a path deemed fruitful by the teacher. Intentions are generally good; the prime objective is simultaneously to introduce what others write, say, and show while drawing out connections through the use of language. Nonetheless, the inherent power is always present, and it is exercised through the use of language. The teacher is the authority; she or he knows things that the students do not know, and is (ideally) attempting to enhance the students' bodies of knowledge. There tends to be, then, some deference on the parts of students. With undergraduate students the deference can manifest itself as assuming what the teacher says is a statement of what is, or it can manifest itself as quietly revolting against the implicit authority with which the teacher speaks.

If we accept that the relationship between teachers and students is at least partly symbolic (that is, the communication that takes places involves the exchange of symbols), the examination of symbolic actions is possible. Suppose Teacher A speaks *at* a class, not really concerned with dialogic communication. This teacher tends to expound, and the responsibility of the students is to absorb. One aspect of the symbolic action in the class is students' perception that they need not be on hand; the class is little more than a performance. To what extent is this teacher accepted by students as a legitimate source of cultural production ("cultural production" defined here as not just learning, but thinking about and accepting the way course topics are given shape, form, and significance)? The power that concerns such a teacher may be described as similar to the power of an actor over an audience in one particular way; attention is the preferred symbolic response. Suppose Teacher B begins a course with a rich discussion of what the course is intended to accomplish, along with how and for whom. This teacher converses with the students, asks questions, looks for analogies in students' experiences, and checks for understanding. Students are not mere receptacles, they are engaged in putting pieces together, with connecting what, when, and how with why. To what extent is *this* teacher accepted as a legitimate source of cultural production? The two examples are extreme illustrations of the exercises of power that Pierre Bourdieu (1991) observes. In between the two may be the functional incorporation of dialogue (which can contribute to legitimacy), but towards an end that is colored by the teacher's desire (conscious or not) to lead students to see the world as the teacher does. The shared community, what Bourdieu refers to as the construction of a linguistic community—even if it is shaped by a teacher's vision, can make the exercise of domination more palatable because it is more transparent (p. 46).

Cultural production can also be very positive and is a commitment for colleges and universities. The processes used need not be rife with dominating ideologies, especially if teachers are sensitized to the possibility of domination. For one thing, a teacher could relinquish some control over what Bourdieu (1989) calls "the mechanisms of reproduction" (p. 105). The mechanisms of reproduction can be opened by questioning any existing orthodoxy, not merely (or not even) to overthrow the orthodoxy, but to achieve the ethical goals of rhetoric that Wayne Booth (2004; see Chapter 2) argues for. A goal is to insist that an orthodoxy's legitimacy (in particular, legitimacy in reason, in openness, and in method) be reaffirmed through critical scrutiny. Orthodoxy does not emanate from any single ideology; any political, social, cultural, or economic stance can create and maintain orthodox positions on the matters it deems central. Critical thinking is sensitive to *how* viewpoints have persisted, not simply *what* those viewpoints are. The libraries' instruction program is an opportunity to introduce students to the evaluation of claims and stances on their merits and not because some informational source says so. [As I have mentioned, the official information literacy documents, as well as a considerable amount of commentary on information literacy constitutes orthodoxy. The recurrence of the ACRL Standards in some form—within course syllabi and institutional statements—could demonstrate the power of the word. The focus in courses and instructional sessions on particular elements (especially searching for, finding, and making some use of information) represents a more tacit orthodoxy. The professional discourse and professional forums can be places for the scrutiny just called for.]

I will suggest here that the syllabus is a kind of cultural production. Not only does it relate the common items, such as course description, objectives, requirements, calendar, and assessment, it communicates the intention of the course. By this I mean the intention that the instructor has for the course's existence and for the change the course will make in students. Both are vital and should be explicit, not just in the mind of the teacher, but for the students. There will be numerous details that form the design of a course, but the syllabus can make clear the reason for the course. The following is a possible outline for a syllabus and an attempt to make intention explicit:

Syllabus Outline

    A.   Course title (this may seem like an obvious inclusion, but as has been stated, the name of the course is a powerful communicative tool.)

    B.   Course description (there will probably a required catalog description of the course, but it may not be sufficient; if the required description is too brief, this is an opportunity to expand and clarify.)

       1. The teacher's statement of the reason for the course' existence (this may vary from instructor to instructor, but it does require every teacher to give thought to the reason why the course is offered.)

       2. Description of the course content (this may be the elements of the standard description.)

       3. Summary of what the course will mean to students (the summary can be a statement of how students will think about what others say, write, and show. It could be something like, "After this course you will never think the same way about what you read while here at [College or University]. You will begin to question everything.")

    C.   Course objectives (this is also usually required in syllabi, but the language used can be formulaic. State in clear terms how students will be affected by what happens in the course: "Every student will be able to frame questions in ways meaningful to course assignments, papers, and her or his own curiosity.")

    D.   Course calendar (it is necessary to provide a schedule of class meetings and the topics for each meeting. Few syllabi detail precisely how the class sessions relate to one another: "Last week we discussed the structure of databases; this week we will delve into how those databases comprise extended conversations.")

    E.   Assessment (all syllabi have descriptions of assignments and exams, as well as including the grading scale. Few transcend this description to communicate the intended meaning of the assignments in ways that will connect the exercises to knowledge and skill that can be used throughout students' academic programs.)

    This kind of syllabus might serve for a semester-long course; what about one or two sessions offered within the course of faculty member somewhere on campus? There is little or no need for items A, D, and E. Items B and C, though, in shortened form, can provide the aim of the instructional session. Purpose is still an essential element of the session, just as the faculty member's location of each topic in the course is important. There are still some goals to be achieved as part of the session, and these should be communicated clearly to the students (and first to the faculty member). Also, as is the case of a course syllabus, the background information enables the students to comprehend that, just because a librarian is speaking to them (instead of the teacher of their course), what is said is integral to the course. The librarian is providing students with assistance that can help them succeed. Further, what follows in this chapter can be employed in sessions offered in faculty members' courses; effective and meaningful communication is no less important because the interaction does not last throughout the semester.

Speech in the Classroom

Moving on to more concrete employment of language in the academic world, the speech in the classroom is an essential determinate of learning. An examination of the language used in any course or instructional session (including at one's own library) can be revealing. In librarianship, as in any profession, a considerable amount of technical language is used. I will not refer to such languages as "jargon;" it is necessary for any field or profession to develop linguistic tactics that lend consistency and specificity to communication. The main shortcoming of any technical language is that it tends to be developed and used *within* the field or profession, albeit with reason. One of the many functions of educational programs is to acculturate students to the prevailing communication practices. Those outside the field or profession are not acculturated in this way. My recommendation regarding this particular use of language is not to abandon the technical language, but to take care defining terms for students in courses and instructional sessions. Make as few assumptions as possible when it comes to students' familiarity with technical language. Once again, the inquiry conducted by Rachel Naismith and Joan Stein (1989) can provide guidance in the design of courses and the speech in the classes. Their work illustrates what students tend not to be acquainted with, and can suggest some specific terms to define (and whose definitions to reinforce). For example, they find that "citation" can be misunderstood; the word, though, is used beyond librarianship and is likely to be mentioned by teachers in other courses. It is an efficient term, and students can benefit by adopting and using it.

The incorporation of technical language in classroom speech can be almost unconscious; after all, it is part of our communicative action every day. The language is so ingrained (in librarianship and in all fields and professions) that users think in terms of the language. The cognitive abilities of the students are not equipped, at the time they are introduced to it, to enable thought in such language. Words and terms can have other meanings outside the profession or could have such limited technical meaning as to be foreign to students. Let us step back for a moment. As is stated above, what happens in the classroom turns on language. The language contributes to the relationships that teachers and students have. It may well be that the relationship is given insufficient consideration by some teachers. It is not only librarians, but teachers in a number of fields who employ an information-processing model. In a simplified form this model signals the imparting of information that is selected by the teacher, and the presumed development of a schema by students. The context for the information transmission and its intended utility is generated by the teacher. Students' schemata, as a result, are shaped by the context created by someone else. Assignments and exams likewise presume schemata that are defined by the teacher. In short, the relationship established by the information-processing model is one of distance between the teacher and the students.

The operation of schemata will be discussed in greater detail in the next chapter; the communication in the classroom, though, is determinate of the teacher-student relationship. Pierre Bourdieu and Jean-Claude Passeron (1994) write, "What makes linguistic misunderstanding in the teaching relationship so serious is that it goes beyond the superficialities of jargon to the operation of a code" (p. 4). The misunderstanding they speak of is exacerbated when the code is *sub rosa*. Bourdieu and Passeron (1994) write further, "Communication can only be regarded as pedagogical when every effort is made to eliminate the faulty 'signals' inherent in an incomplete knowledge of the code and to transmit the code in the most efficient way" (p. 5). The analysis of course content (above) shows that some courses include explicit effort to describe the code and to help students assimilate the code. When most successful, courses frame the code of information-carrying packages (the library's catalog, databases, the Web) into the broader academic code—the systematic structure of teaching across the campus. "Database" for example, is a name for something that can open a door to journal articles and the things the authors of the articles say. More course descriptions, though, do not demonstrate code sharing. The discourse in the classroom may accomplish such sharing, but what is communicated via libraries' Web sites may not admit to the sharing. As is the case with technical language generally, the existence of a code is not constitutive of distance or of an ineffectual teacher-student relationship. It does represent a discursive and communicative challenge, one that cannot be ignored. The challenge is also reflected in Booth's charge to speakers to create understanding.

Michel Foucault adopts a somewhat more radical stance on discursive practices. Many people interpret Foucault as representing extreme postmodernism—destruction of the grand narratives that have typified modern society; denial that knowledge and truth are possible; abandonment of history. I believe these interpretations are off-base; in fact, Foucault's voice is much more moderate in its aim, even as it is critical in its analysis. In *Archaeology of Knowledge* (1972) Foucault claims that a book is more than its material substance (paper and ink); it is one contextual element in a complex discursive pastiche that is formed by historical and contemporary practices (pp. 22-30). This point is very important for libraries' instructional programs. Any document (in the broadest sense) that is retrieved does not (cannot) stand alone; it is part of a much larger discussion that has been woven through time, not necessarily in a strictly linear manner. The references that accompany scholarly works constitute one particular indicator of the larger discussion. An author relies on what others have said as part of the formation of her or his work. In some cases the journal (defined as the contents of what it has published since its beginning) is also an indicator of the scope and breadth of the conversation. The journal's content may not be entirely self-referential (every paper will not relate directly to every other paper), but there is a unity that may be explicit in the stated editorial policy.

There is another aspect of Foucault's thought that is relevant to instruction. As is noted above, a number of courses and instructional sessions include explanation of the process of production, particularly of scholarly texts. For example, the refereeing process may be described. The description tends to focus on mechanics. One example is the tutorial developed by librarians at Rutgers University (http://www.rci.rutgers. edu/~estec/tutorials/scholarly.htm). The descriptions are accurate, but incomplete. The traditional media of production are also forces of control that operate within a social structure; some things get published and some do not. In the world of scholarship a piece of work has a better chance of being published if it fits clearly within epistemological, methodological, and even teleological traditions. For example, if the referees used by a particular editor are all senior faculty members who have developed their own research programs, one can ask if they will be receptive to programs that challenge those programs. In short, the senior faculty, as referees, may operate with certain (exclusive) traditions. Foucault (1972) depicts the forces of traditions:

> Certainly, as a proposition, the division between true and false is neither arbitrary, nor modifiable, nor institutional, nor violent. Putting the question in different terms, however—asking what has been, what still is, throughout our discourse, this will to truth which has survived throughout so many centuries of our history; or if we ask what is, in its very general form, the kind of division governing our will to knowledge—then we may well discern something like a system of exclusion (historical, modifiable, institutionally constraining) in the process of development (p. 218).

His prose is a bit dense, but what he says is that the cultural and societal development and determination of discourse is not as open, either as we all think it is or even that its producers may be fully cognizant of. Truth itself is not at issue; what is presented as true, what is offered as representing knowledge, is controlled. The control, as Foucault (1972) says, "is both reinforced and accompanied by whole strata of practices such as pedagogy—naturally—the book-system, publishing, libraries, such as the learned societies in the past, and laboratories today. But it is probably even more profoundly accompanied by the manner in which knowledge is employed in a society, the way in which it is exploited, divided and, in some ways, attributed" (p. 219).

These are disquieting thoughts; it is natural for anyone to resist Foucault's charges. He is convincing, though, in his explanation of the human tendencies that lead people to adhere to traditions, to deny challenges to historically held opinions, to dismiss ideas that run counter to what one believes to be true. Some instructional objectives in libraries' programs are to evaluate information and to incorporate it into one's work. Many courses and sessions provide guidance as to examination of authority, reliability of the publisher, and other surface elements. Some libraries have developed tutorials, sometimes to be incorporated into the library's course and sometimes to be used for specific purposes (including for presentation as part of a course, introductory or advanced, in some department). The University of Hawaii Libraries offers a tutorial on evaluation that covers such things (http://library. kcc.hawaii.edu/external/hookele/susan/evaluating.html). The following is one excerpt from the tutorial:

Which one of the following would you consider the most authoritative source for *the pros and cons of irradiating food*:

a. Good food you can't get. (food irradiation) Larry Katzenstein. Reader's Digest, July 1993 v143 n855 p43(5).

b. Irradiation to prevent foodborne illness. (From the Assistant Secretary for Health. US Public Health Service) Philip R. Lee. JAMA, The Journal of the American Medical Association, July 27, 1994 v272 n4 p261(1).

c. Fruit irradiation (editorial). Honolulu Star Bulletin, 01 Jan 1997 A2.

d. Gamma rays have a glowing future. (Isomedix Inc.) Herbert E. Meyer. Fortune, May 4, 1981 v103 p201 (5).

The critical thinking that is also sometimes mentioned as an objective seldom receives substantive treatment. It is the critical treatment of what others say, write, and show that Foucault hints at. In actuality, Foucault is investigating current practice in light of historical contexts. At one point he (1972) writes,

> Education may well be, as of right, the instrument whereby every individual, in a society like our own, can gain access to any kind of discourse. But we well know that in its distribution, in what it permits and in what it prevents, it follows the well-trodden battle-lines of social conflict. Every educational system is a political means of maintaining or of modifying the appropriation of discourse, with the knowledge and the powers it carries with it (p. 227).

The "is" in the last sentence is very important in his observation. There is indeed a system of control at work in the production of the content packages (books, journals, official publications, etc.); producers decide what will be disseminated and what cannot be. How do libraries' instructional programs address the system of control?

The above examination of courses and sessions, along with Hrycaj's study, demonstrate that libraries' programs concentrate on *how* the system works. The coverage of search protocols, the elements of records, the means of combining search terms, and other matters is fairly extensive. Moreover, again, the coverage is necessary; students have to know how the system works. Understanding of the system's technical operations is not sufficient, though. The understanding enables students to retrieve works, but it does not help them comprehend how the things get into production. In another essay, "What Is an Author," Foucault (1998) says that an author is not simply the writer of the text that bears his or her name; the author also creates possibilities. For example, when Einstein published his special theory of relativity he altered the way physicists spoke of their field. Following Foucault's point, Einstein not only made a contribution to the conversation through his own writings, but also through influence on the turn of the conversation. Not all authors have the profound impact that, say, Einstein, Marx, and Freud have had on the conversations in their fields and beyond. Many authors have lesser impact, though, and influence (sometimes subtly) the paths of discourse. Every professional librarian may be able to recall some work by some author that not only prompted a different way of thinking about a topic, but also a different way of speaking about it. This idea of Foucault's is one specific example of the nature of dialogic communication.

I realize that Foucault's writing may not fit well in a libraries' course (his prose is not really suited to lower-division undergraduate students), but he suggests examples and analogies that can be used in a class. The discussion of production should accompany the more general description of the peer-review process. An illustration of control that can fit readily into a class session is mention of the acceptance rates of journals. In the social sciences, acceptance rates are generally in the range of 35-40%. The rates can vary widely from title to title, in part depending on the prestige of the journals. The American Psychological Association reports on data related to its journals (see, for example, http://www.apa.org/journals/statistics/2005operations.pdf). The acceptance rate for

Journal of Experimental Psychology: Learning, Memory, and Cognition is 33%, but the rate for the *Journal of Abnormal Psychology* is only 6%. Students can be asked to speculate why the majority of the submissions to these journals are rejected. The possibilities certainly include flaws in the work submitted—methodological problems, insufficient data, analytical errors, and so on. The exercise of control may be needed as a means to keep flawed and erroneous work from confusing the discourse. Control is not necessarily deleterious, but it can have some unfortunate consequences. As was pointed out earlier, one could ask: Is it possible that referees who reviewed some works just did not like them? Could the rejected works have challenged the status quo of the fields in some way? The principal point of such a class discussion is to let students know that production is a human action, influenced by social, as well as intellectual, factors. The factors are complex and may not even be fully apparent to those involved in the process (some faculty members themselves may not fully apprehend the complexity). An awareness of the phenomena that Foucault describes does not, and should not lead one to extreme skepticism regarding what is published. In fact, teachers should tell students emphatically that the exercise of control does not render everything (or even a sizable minority) of published works unreliable. What Foucault reveals is that the control and the will cannot be ignored.

Following Foucault, there is no formula to be applied that can provide an automatic evaluation of people's ideas. Ideas are not physical objects, and authors' affiliations, journal titles, and publishers—while important—are not sufficient for evaluation. Ideas and thoughts are not well suited to quantitative kinds of evaluation; a more phenomenological means is needed. The customary elements of surface evaluation can only be used as aggregative means; that is, an author's affiliation presumes that some affiliations are necessarily more reliable than others. Does this mean that an author from Harvard is more reliable than an author from East Texas State University? Such evaluation does not delve into what the authors say and how they say it. The construction of ideas and the rhetoric within which the ideas are expressed are integral to knowledge growth. Operationally, evaluation entails weighing differences and similarities, consistencies and inconsistencies. In a radio program about training intelligence analysts in the U.S. someone mentions that there is a kind of critical questioning needed for the analysis.

An example given is an analyst presented with seventeen documents; whether they came from one single source or seventeen different sources makes a difference in analysis. The analysts' training is geared to awaken people to the many factors that affect production and dissemination of works. The acumen that the analysts acquire is only one basic form of critical awareness; it is used here to illustrate the practical application of cognitive abilities that can be gained relatively early in life. A similar kind of critical questioning can accompany class discussion on journal publishing. A single source will usually not provide sufficient evidence—empirical, logical, or rhetorical—to reach a sound conclusion on some matter. Sources may be in disagreement; they must be evaluated according to substantive, not merely surface, criteria.

Sharing the Code

If we start with the premise that a code does exist and that successful learning depends on students comprehending the code, we can move forward to an investigation of *how* instruction can accomplish the objective. The first step involves reflection; every teacher should become aware of the linguistic strategies, or rhetoric, he or she employs. The obvious place to begin is with "information literacy." The term has already been critiqued; this critique offers some suggestions for reflection. If one intends to base instruction on the Standards, then they must be decoded. First, the Standards must be clear—conceptually as well as linguistically—to the teacher. The emerging clarity should inform the syllabus. The syllabus is probably the first speech act between teacher and students, and it is here that mutual understanding can have its beginning.

The "action" component of phenomenological cognitive action is emphasized in speech act theory, but the other two elements are present. The conjoining of the three cannot be overstated; when it comes to sharing a code the three are most effective when integrated. At the outset it is important to admit that the code that is employed as a single system. Semiotics was introduced in the critique of "information," but its application is extensive. Semiotics in simplified form can be most useful for the present discussion. As was said in the previous context ("information"), the key to expression or utterance is the signifier—it is the sign or sign complex that is overt (and can be straightforward as a statement made in class or the instructions for an assignment). To use an example already described, students might be asked how frequently they use AND, OR, and NOT in searching. "AND" is a signifier; the signified, in technical language, could be "the concurrence of the terms on each side of the operator in a search string." Since that signified is technical, it may not be automatically shared between teacher and students. If the technical signified remains implicit (that is, it is not explained in terms of a shared code), the signifier AND may be empty for students. An outcome of implicit communication of signs is described by Bourdieu and Passeron (1994): "if the teacher sticks to the linguistic requirements that at present govern his discourse, rather than submitting his language to the demands of explicitness, he prevents students as they really are from meeting his requirements and continues to saddle himself with contradictory expectations" (p. 23). Without the effort to ensure clarity, confusion is much more likely.

The aim of sharing the code is learning. Clarity, intelligibility, and communicability are more specific objectives. Taking a cue from Booth's (2004) "listening-rhetoric," one way to look at a course might be to envision a series of potential obstacles. The teacher can ask which of the potential obstacles can be avoided, and how. If we include all possibilities, we can begin with the course title. Titles such as "Information Literacy" and "Library Instruction" are indicative of language that may not be shared. When people in the academy talk about language, they can hardly avoid Ludwig Wittgenstein's work. His ideas on language involve the incorporation of a game model. Language as game entails rules that people devise. The rules, for those who play the game together, are imbedded; they become imbedded in speech and action. For those who do not share the rules, not only is understandability difficult, the causes of the problem are not readily apparent. Imagine children who have grown up together in a neighborhood who invent a game they call "football." In the past they invented and refined the rules for this game, and the rules are not similar to those for any other game. Suppose, too, that the children in this neighborhood have never played American football or soccer. One day two kids from other places move to the neighborhood. One has grown up playing American football, but knows nothing of the neighborhood game or of soccer. The other has grown up playing soccer, but knows nothing of the neighborhood game or American football. All of the children call the game they are familiar with "football." When the new kids try to play, they are confused by the game; the kids from the neighborhood cannot understand what goes wrong, since the new kids say they know how to play football.

Jürgen Habermas (2001) offers an explication of the problem just described, transferred to communication: "If we take a language game to be a system of rules according to which utterances that can yield a consensus can be formed, then, according to Wittgenstein, the grammar of a language game can be exhibited but cannot be expressed in the form of a theoretical account" (p. 53). There is no need to delve into the totality of Wittgenstein's theory of language, but his images of language games are useful here. He says that the rules of language are arbitrary; let us alter that to say that the rules of a code are arbitrary. To change slightly what Wittgenstein says, the rule of a code are not natural, if "natural" means being determined by a particular end. What might be referred to in an instructional setting as a "citation" is not so named because "citation" denotes a physical or metaphysical thing. For example, the same thing called a "citation" could also be referred to as a "reference" or a "bibliographic entry." To illustrate his point Wittgenstein (1974) says, "You cook badly if you are guided in your cooking by rules other than the right ones; but if you follow other rules than those of chess you are playing another game" (p. 184). Understanding, in the classroom, depends on the teacher and the students agreeing to the rules of the game; in the academic world this usually entails introducing students explicitly to a set of rules that have already been established.

There is a particular implication that language, as Wittgenstein talks about it, has for instructional programs. Beyond the explanation of the technical language, there is the language that is needed in the totality of the question framing-search strategy-retrieval-evaluation-use process. The language must be introduced to all students as such. This kind of language use is entwined with cultural production and we may wonder how diverse culture can be. Habermas (1998) provides a working definition of "culture:" "Culture is what I call the stock of knowledge from which the participants in communication, in reaching understanding with one another with regard to something, supply themselves with interpretations" (p. 248). To break down his definition a bit, the body of knowledge that is shared is the source of potential interpretations. Code sharing is related to the body of knowledge; let us say that content (knowledge) and expression (code) contribute to culture. As librarians, we share a body of knowledge regarding organization of information, structures of information containers or packages, the body of knowledge transmitted through the containers, and the populations that the library is intended to serve. We also share the code used to express particulars about each of the above elements ("MARC record," "truncation," "reference interview"). Librarianship (that is, the collective of professionals) can be seen as a culture.

A question begs to be asked: What is the culture of undergraduate students? It is a serious question, the answer to which could be very helpful to all who teach undergraduates. The first part of an answer would entail comprehending that there is not likely to be a single culture (using Habermas's definition). The body or stock of knowledge would likely include aspects of popular culture, music, games, television, movies, YouTube, Facebook, etc. Cultures have to be acknowledged; they can be used as connectors among students and between students and the academy. Culture, for Habermas (1998), is not the limit of social interaction; he also defines "society:" "Society consists of the legitimate orders by way of which the participants in communication regulate their affiliations to social groups and safeguard solidarity" (p. 248). Taking a generous view of the definition, mutually acceptable regulations—not so much to control as to enable—enhance what is shared and promotes understanding. Society is perpetuated by means of communicative action. Habermas separates his definitions from more frequently used political ones (that address the instrumental interactions of people in an ordered and confined society). He connects his definitions to the phenomenological concept of lifeworld. Lifeworld is, at its core, an individual phenomenon through which each of us sees and interprets what is around us and communicates with one another. The "components of the lifeworld should not be conceived of as systems constituting environments for one another; they remain entwined with one another via the common medium of everyday language (Habermas, 1998, p. 250).

Rhetoric

The preceding section brings some essential elements of communication to the fore. It opens the door to more pointed discussion of rhetoric (it was mentioned above that colleges and universities may have courses that nominally include rhetoric, but its importance is not fully recognized). Rhetoric has not been ignored in the professional literature, but it has definitely not held a prominent place in librarians' discourse. Jeanne

Davidson and Carole Ann Crateau (2000) have written perhaps the most sustained piece involving rhetoric in instruction. Their suggestion for integration is very important and should be employed in all courses:

> Ideally, students interact at three levels with the schol-
> arly conversation. First, they become familiar with the
> discipline, "eavesdropping" on the scholarly conversa-
> tion. Second, they choose a focus for their research
> and writing, "entering" the conversation. Third, they
> form their own opinions and prepare to persuade oth-
> ers of their ideas, "engaging" in the conversation. The
> rhetorical strategies used at each of these levels vary,
> requiring appropriate instructional support (p. 248).

The three levels could be called rhetorical/cognitive, since they entail thinking and speaking on topics that require exploration. Mark Emmons and Wanda Martin (2002) also embrace the notion of engaging in conversation, though not quite as directly as do Davidson and Crateau. They operationalize the rhetorical dimension in a rubric designed to depict ideal and actual student performance. In putting rhetoric into operation they tend to apply some instrumental measures of success, such as "all sources clearly related to topic" for assessment of content relevance (p. 552). Both pairs of authors draw from Carol Kuhlthau's work, although it can be argued that her emphasis on a linear approach becoming informed reduces the complex cognitive process of entering and engaging in scholarly rhetoric to rote procedures (i.e., Kuhlthau (2004) obscures her exploration of seeking meaning by presenting a normative model that provides no room for iterative processes, let alone nonlinear ones).

Of primary importance here is the recognition that "rhetoric" is not used in the popular pejorative way. Rhetoric is not limited to eloquence or decoration; it is not simply a means to persuade through style. It is also a means to discovery and a tool in truth-seeking. Wayne Booth's (2004) straightforward definition of rhetoric was introduced in the last chapter; the welfare of the audience is an important concern. Booth is quick to affirm that factual knowledge is important, but that its utility is limited to the context—intellectual, social, political, etc.—in what the facts exist and are reported. By the same token, libraries' instructional programs *must* include treatment of database structure, search protocols, and the like, but not separated from the intellectual purpose of engaging in the conversation. In the educational setting there will be conflict over ideas; some will accept particular ideas and others will reject them. Rhetoric can help all teachers to achieve educational goals in two ways: (1) the class discussion is constructively developed so that speakers are attended to and a civil discourse ensues, and (2) rhetoric enables students to weigh arguments on their merits. Booth (2004) summarizes the second point superbly:

Any nation is in trouble if its citizens are not trained for crucial response to the flood of misinformation poured over them daily. A citizenry not habituated to thoughtful argument about public affairs, but rather trained to "believe everything supporting my side" and "disbelieve everything supporting the bad side," is no longer a citizenry but a house of gullibles (p. 89).

The emphasis on rhetoric places something of a burden on teachers. Using Booth's language, teachers should be sensitive to what he calls "rhetorology," or the quest for common ground. In part the responsibility entails avoiding relativism and recognizing that the search for truth is legitimate and necessary. This is not to say that it is an easy search; disciplinary efforts to define knowledge include employing rhetoric both to frame problems and to assert answers. That rhetorical employment cannot be ignored and is part of students' education. Different academic fields establish norms for argument, evidence, and validity. The *concepts* of argument, evidence, and validity are inescapable, though. Booth's (2004) admonition sums up the necessity for, and the importance of, rhetoric: "What is inescapable is that underlying all our differences about what makes good communication there is one deep standard: agreement that whatever the dispute, whatever the language standards, communication can be improved by *listening to the other side, and then listening even harder to one's own responses* [emphasis in original]" (p. 21).

Mikhail Bakhtin, Dialogue, and Instruction

We are working through some difficult and challenging conceptual suggestions here, but I do hope the background assists in framing the new foundation. An even more complex manifestation of phenomenological cognitive action centers on the idea of dialogism, and is related to Booth's conception of rhetoric. This is not the most elegant word, but it refers to the particular ideas about phenomenology expressed by the Russian philosopher and critic, Mikhail Bakhtin. Bakhtin's (1986, 1993) work on speech has quite a lot in common with Searle's speech acts. That is, it is not limited to conversation, fiction, or other particular forms of expression. For Bakhtin, dialogue was at the center of speech. This is not to say that all speech is dialogic; in his later years he admitted that much scientific communication is in the form of a monologue. Monologic communication could be conceived as the practice of "talking at." Such communication is indifferent to the existence of a reader or a hearer. It tends to be an utterance that suggests no question, or indeed no response of any kind. For Bakhtin (1986), dialogue is the primary way that consciousness manifests itself, even for the individual alone (we can think about some fiction in which a character engages in an internal monologue). The dialogic consciousness is much more closely connected to phenomenology as I am defining it here than it is to cognition; because of this, the discussion fits best with this section on communication. Bakhtin's main concern (this is a theme that runs through his writings) is the manner by which a person can know or come to understand non-literal things. By non-literal I mean objects or ideas that require some interpretation.

There are some definite implications of dialogue for instruction (all instruction). The primary reason for the failure of some lectures to foster learning is that they are (obviously) monologues. These lectures are delivered by and for the speaker; the language used is a shared language only by accident. (This notion hearkens back to what Bourdieu says about classroom communication.) Not all lectures are absolute monologues; the structure of the lecture, as well as its delivery, can be designed to create sharing. For instance, multiple examples, analogues, or metaphors may be offered so that the experiences and knowledge of the audience members allow for engagement. The lecture form itself, though, has limited dialogic possibilities. So Plato used Socratic dialogues to present, not only statements, but counter-statements, questions, challenges, and so on. The pedagogical styles point to the complexity of dialogue. Of particular interest (since all teachers are charged with enabling students to increase their knowledge) is the role of dialogue as an epistemological strategy. I use the word "strategy" here deliberately and choose not to use the word "tool" because dialogue is itself a phenomenon, an event. As such it can only be engaged in as a path to knowledge. If I speak to you using linguistic or rhetorical tools, I am bent on manipulating your response. Dialogue entails critical perception that is not predetermined (even though it can be guided, as Socrates did).

The fundamental concept of dialogue carries an insistence that the relationship between teacher and student (and student and teacher, and student and student) is one of "I and Thou" (that way of expressing the relationship of self and other comes primary from Emmanuel Levinas; see 1979). In the parlance of phenomenology it is a relationship of otherness. I cannot stress this point emphatically enough. The relationship suggests the foundational difference between the natural sciences and the human sciences. It is possible, for the most part, to comprehend, for example, Einstein's equation ($E = mc^2$) because each variable is purely physical—without consciousness or volition. Because an other self does embody consciousness and will, knowledge of others is limited. A source of the limitation is the intentionality (another phenomenological concept) that is part of our thoughts and actions. The limitation, while real, is far from absolute, though. In Bakhtin's (1993) own (somewhat abstruse) words, "To understand an object is to understand my ought in relation to it (the attitude or position I ought to take in relation to it), that is, to understand it in relation to me myself in once-occurrent Being-as-event, and that presupposes my answerable participation, and not an abstracting from myself" (p. 18). Understanding, that is, involves a responsibility. When the "object" is the teaching-learning relationship there are responsibilities on both sides. The responsibility is to use one's own experiences and body of knowledge as a means to create the possibility for action. A learner asks, What *can* I do, as well as, What *should* I do? Unfortunately, some have interpreted Bakhtin as paving the way for relativism. The dialogic nature of knowledge does not necessarily entail that knowledge is socially situated. As Booth (2004) says, there are non-contingent realities, realities that do not depend on human expression or even perception. The cognitive implications for a non-relativist stance will be explored in the next chapter and the discussion of cognition.

This a good time to place dialogue squarely in the context of the instructional situation. If a course aims to fulfill the imperatives of ACRL Standard Two, then access, searching, and retrieval cannot be abstractions. They cannot be separated from the *reasons* for searching and retrieving. The act of searching itself is not "Being-as-event;" there is no inherent relationship between the conscious, knowing person and the mere act of searching. Bakhtin (1986) addresses this point quite directly:

> The transcription of thinking in the human sciences is always the transcription of a special kind of dialogue: the complex interactions between the *text* (the object of study and reflection) and the created, framing *context* (questioning, refuting, and so forth) in which the scholar's cognizing and evaluating thought takes place. This is the meeting of two texts—of the ready-made and the reactive text being created—and, consequently, the meeting of two subjects and two authors (pp. 106-07).

What Bakhtin realizes is that, in the act of searching and retrieving, one does not retrieve a physical object; one communicates with a text, with an utterance. The utterance—say, an article written by someone, that a person can read as part of the action of framing and asking a question—is an intentional creation. The author had a plan in writing the article in precisely the way it was written. Bakhtin (1986) wisely illustrates other challenges that are integral to libraries' instructional programs. He says that the notion of context is itself complex. In the terms of instruction, while a student may read an article in the context of the question as originally framed, she also reads it in the context of the other articles read, and her responses to them (p. 146). An act of reading (or hearing, or viewing) is not a discrete event; it is a component of Being on a larger scale.

Bakhtin's conception of dialogue as a path to knowledge admits to some challenges to dialogic communication. As was already noted, communication can be monologic, can ignore the I-Thou relationship. Furthermore, the I-Thou relationship can be constructed in particular ways to make texts either accessible or inaccessible. An example of a technical paper can illustrate that the author may indeed have an intended audience, but that audience is a limited group of specialists. An assumption may be made, for instance, regarding the mathematical knowledge of readers. For undergraduate students, the introduction of dialogue can serve the purpose simultaneously of removing feelings of inadequacy brought on by the misperception that the author intended to engage in dialogue with them when he did not, and of augmenting students' critical perception of intentional dialogue and the many purposes they may serve. All of these observations on dialogue also fit the classroom itself. Teachers will have to understand dialogue and employ it, both epistemologically and ethically in the classroom. The dialogue ideally begins from the standpoint of employing practical reason to the relationship of people and texts. The teacher is, in a real sense, an author. The teacher's is usually the first utterance in the class, so the relationship is begun by the teacher. Bakhtin's complete works demonstrate that, even though an author-reader-text exists, dialogue is possible.

Not only is dialogue possible, it is essential in an educational endeavor. To repeat, dialogic communication is not a slippery slope to relativism; the educational goal is understanding through mutual expression and attention. It is not reactionary to argue against unlimited difference in favor of quests for knowledge and truth, even in foundational student experiences like libraries' instructional programs. Paul Ricoeur (1992) points teachers in the right direction in urging everyone to avoid the valorizing of difference, "which, finally, makes all differences indifferent, to the extent that it makes all discussion useless" (p. 286). If we do sink into relativism, there is not only no resolution to any dispute or conflict, there is no conviction that one alternative may be superior to others. In the context of libraries' instructional programs, necessity of conviction translates to the evaluation of content, of rhetorical expressions. If we base programs on the necessity of evaluation, then there has to be a mechanism for evaluation in the sense of discriminating among expressions.

Pathways to Knowledge

The content of a libraries' course is bound to be a rather difficult design challenge. The challenge includes rational, social, and disciplinary elements. Paths to knowledge differ from field to field, but goals of exploration and discourse tend to be fairly consistent. That is, whatever a student's eventual major, that student will be taught particular ways of reading, viewing, and thinking about what people say, write, and show. Faculty members in physics will present one way of accumulating and evaluating evidence, of making claims, and of examining the objects of study. Faculty members in history will present something quite different. Almost all faculty attempt to communicate to students the objectives of learning and knowledge growth. Teachers in libraries' instructional programs might take a cue from René Descartes (1989), who developed a set of rules for himself:

> The first was never to accept anything for true which I did not clearly know to be such; that is to say, carefully avoid precipitancy and prejudice, and to comprise nothing more in my judgment than what was presented to my mind so clearly and distinctly as to exclude all ground of doubt.

The second, to divide each of the difficulties under examination into as many parts as possible, and as might be necessary for its adequate solution.

The third, to conduct my thoughts in such order that, by commencing with objects the simplest and easiest to know, I might ascend by little and little, and, as it were, step by step, to the knowledge of the more complex; assigning in thought a certain order even to those objects which in their own nature do not stand in a relation of ascendance and sequence.

And the last, in every case to make enumerations so complete, and reviews so general, that I might be assured that nothing was omitted (p. 21).

Descartes, as is evident from his own words, placed rationality above all else. I am not suggesting that teachers adopt Descartes's strict criteria wholesale; some of his rules are more applicable to the instructional programs than others. The third is probably the most useful here. In presenting complex ideas and the speech in which those ideas are framed, progressing from simple to difficult is likely to be an effective strategy. The second rule can also be useful for an undergraduate class. Many complex topics are comprised of parts that can be examined on their own. The potential drawback of this rule is that some topics' parts are closely interrelated; this is not say that the parts cannot be studied independently of one another, but synthesis will be vital to a complete understanding. The primary drawback of Descartes's rationality rests in the first rule, which may be impossible to follow to the extent that he intends. His definition of knowledge is limited to the explicit, to the natural. It avoids the discursive or the rhetorical. That limitation is serious, so while the rules can offer a beginning for teachers, they constitute only one limited pathway to knowledge. In fact, Descartes's ideas of rationality have been challenged, not only by philosophers, but also by social scientists (see, for example, Flyvberg, 2001). For one thing, his method requires reduction to the smallest possible parts. While some reduction is necessary (for instance, a retrieved article can be reduced to the question asked, the methodology, the evidence, and the findings); complex phenomena cannot be effectively reduced beyond a certain extent.

To supplement, rather to replace entirely, Descartes's rules, libraries' instructional programs can add some qualities of thought. For one thing, while Descartes warns against accepting something as true that is actually false, the reverse is also a possible error (accepting the false as true). The latter may be even more common than the former. It is incumbent upon instructional programs to address belief for what it is. A belief can be true or not; a belief can rest in faith or in evidence. In short, belief is not the same as knowledge (to reiterate an earlier point) (see, for example, MacIntyre, 2006). Education is the exploration of beliefs (as well as claims) by means of rigorous scrutiny. This necessarily means that education will, at times, be uncomfortable for students. Not only will topics be difficult, they may be challenging to what students' thought they knew. Descartes's rules may apply well to knowledge of objects, but not so well to knowledge of relations. Paul Ricoeur (2005) wisely reminds us that a major challenge for education is developing an understanding of "being-in-the-world." That expression is a melding of the physical, objective world with personal, and interpersonal, perception of the world and ourselves in it. Being-in-the-world is a vital concept when considering framing questions, searching for, retrieving, and interpreting works. Meaning is not something that is likely to be self-evident. In the next chapter the conversation turns to the cognitive elements that surround the framing, searching, retrieving, and interpreting, as well as finding meaning.

KEY POINTS IN CHAPTER THREE:

➤ Courses offered by libraries may not follow the Standards, and may be limited to the more mechanical or instrumental elements of instruction programs

➤ The syllabus deserves close attention because it is a primary communicative tool between teachers and students (and elements of a syllabus can be employed even in single-session presentations in classes across the curriculum)

➤ Academic speech can become an exclusionary code, so all teachers must take care to enable the clearest and most effective communication

➤ Libraries' instruction—whether full courses or single sessions—frequently address processes of cultural production; both the production within fields such as history or chemistry *and* the production of communication in general might be covered

➤ Librarians are in a special position to ensure that full appreciation of rhetoric, particularly as the search for truth, is incorporated into the classroom

➤ Dialogue (the interrelationship of self and other) is essential for the growth of understanding in students

CHAPTER FOUR

Cognition and Clear Thinking

What is critical thinking? It is frequently mentioned as a goal in elementary, secondary, and higher education. It can be connected to the mundane in the sense that it is vital to making decisions in one's life. More often it is placed in the academic context, and information tends to feature prominently. Critical thinking, as a term, can actually be "unpacked" so that we can see how it fits into instructional programs. The "critical" element is best drawn from critique; that means examining closely to understand the logical, empirical, intersubjective, and moral bases for what is said, written, and shown. The purpose is not necessarily to find fault with claims and statements, but to subject them to careful scrutiny. There are too few models of critique available in popular media and common discourse today. That is a common complaint; it is intended here to illustrate that it is difficult for teachers to provide guides to critique in everyday life. The reasons or causes for the difficulty are beyond the scope of this project; despite the challenge, it is worthwhile seeking any examples of critique that can be found.

The "thinking" part of critical thinking is even more of a challenge. The first three chapters have demonstrated that much attention is paid to constructing content that students should be aware of, as well as suggestions for adjustments to that content. It is now time to explore the cognitive elements of learning. Cognitive science has made great strides towards comprehension of how people think and learn. Also, a considerable amount of that research has been put into practice. There is one shortcoming to some work in cognition (and probably more common in application of cognitive research in fields like education). John Searle (1997) points out that the mistake can arise from a misunderstanding of causation: In our official theories of causation we typically suppose that all causal relations must be between discrete events ordered sequentially in time" (p. 7). Neither Searle nor I deny that there are material causes of actions. Causation, especially when it comes to human action, is likely to be extremely complex. Rather than a simple model—A occurs, and its occurrence directly causes B—there may be a set of interactive, even interdependent or quasi-dependent, causal events. The events may, in some cases, be autonomic; they may, in other cases, be conscious. Examination of learning relates primarily to conscious events. Among cognitive scientists and philosophers of mind there is disagreement whether the events *can* be understood. All teachers need to be aware of some of the ideas that are now circulating in the study of cognition and consciousness. Given the importance of the ways people think, a review of some of the stances regarding cognition will be helpful.

The Materialists

Some thinkers adopt a very strong materialist stance, maintaining that all consciousness and cognition is physical, governed by neuron-chemical factors. One of the most prominent materialists today is Daniel Dennett. He is an engaging, witty, and articulate proponent of materialism and he (2005) is clear about his position: "Consciousness, on this optimistic view, is indeed a wonderful thing, but not *that* wonderful—not too wonderful to be explained using the same concepts and perspectives that have worked elsewhere in biology" (p. 6). He elaborates on the biological foundation of consciousness through his Multiple Drafts model. He (1991) explains, "all varieties of perception—indeed, all varieties of thought or mental activity—are accomplished in the brain by parallel, multitrack processes of interpretation and elaboration of sensory inputs. Information entering the nervous system is under continuous 'editorial revision'" (p. 111). This constitutes a particular version of the information-processing, or computational, model of cognition.

As was mentioned in Chapter One, information processing has both metaphorical and theoretical significance in cognitive science. As metaphor it provides a fairly easily construed depiction of the functions that the brain guides and is guided by. As theory it has literal significance; the brain is not substantively different from a digital computer to the materialists. As computer technology has advanced, both the metaphor and the theory have evolved. Computers are sufficiently ubiquitous (with processing expanded to include design in everyday use) that the analogy is accessible to many people. The increased sophistication of digital processors has developed, in part, following increasing knowledge in neuroscience. Advances in artificial intelligence provide evidence of the sophistication. The array of networking and complex neural processing in the brain resembles advanced digital processing to an extent. Dennett's Multiple Drafts model articulates the complexity of material dynamics that, undoubtedly, does occur in the brain. His model, according to his intention, also illustrates the diffuseness of the phenomenon of consciousness. The impossibility of identifying a single locus for a process (or "thought") and the possibility of tracking a path according to which the process is manifest by no means deflates the material nature of consciousness. Dennett (1991) concludes,

> It turns out that the way to imagine [Dennett's argument] is to think of the brain as a computer of sorts. The concepts of computer science provide the crutches of imagination we need if we are to stumble across the *terra incognita* between our phenomenology [with phenomenology defined specifically as the appearance of things to consciousness, not as the intersubjective, intentional, meaningful aspects of Being that I am taking phenomenology to be] as we know it by "introspection" and our brains as science reveals them to us (p. 433).

As convinced as Dennett is, he still admits that people do have beliefs and desires that, while objective and do not cause human actions, are real. Stronger materialist stances deny even the existence of beliefs, desires, and other mental states. The only things that exist are neurochemical functions that give us misguided and mistaken impressions of the mental states. The name given to this stance is eliminativism, standing for the elimination of common sense causes for our actions in favor of purely physical ones. If you were to say to a friend, "I feel happy today; I'm in a very good mood," the eliminativist would explain your mood away by offering a physical-chemical cause for your behavior. This stance purports to replace one ontology with another; that is, adherents seek to eliminate the presumed existence of mental states with the *actual* existence of concrete phenomena that have causal connections to what goes on in your brain. According to eliminitavists, what you define as real is an illusion. Paul Churchland (1990) is one prominent advocate for eliminativism; the answers to questions of consciousness will be solved by neuroscience. Churchland does not know *how* those questions will be answered, or *what* the answers may be, but he is committed to the theory. As is evident from Dennett's writings, he is at odds with eliminativists when it comes to isolating the neural action that leads to objective mental states. A difficulty with the claims of Dennett and Churchland is actually rather curious, given their materialism. They each *believe*, not just their respective positions, but *in* their respective positions. They offer broad metaphorical justification for their beliefs and exhibit consternation with their detractors and excitement about their beliefs. In other words, they behave in the same ways as those who adopt weaker materialist positions.

The positions of Dennett, Churchland, and others have their bases in some recent work in neuroscience. Developments detailed by, for example, Michael Gazzaniga and Steven Rose (2005) point to a deeper and clearer knowledge of brain functions. It is obvious, because of this scientific progress, that some areas of the brain guide certain functions and that functions are effectively networked. Pathologies have taught neuroscientists an enormous amount; when parts of people's brains are injured or otherwise compromised, it is possible to study effects. Motor functions, speech, and memory, for example, can be located. Gazzaniga (2005) speculates that even interpretation may be localized in the brain. The brain is a genuinely awesome organ. Neuroscience tends to seek deterministic causes of brain functioning; it is an open question, though, whether human action is clearly determined. Given that the very strong materialist position is that there are no mental states, the ontological difference between their belief and the beliefs of those arguing for weaker materialist stances is one of conceptual versus perceptual views of reality. The strong position holds to the conceptual ontology (what *is* can be sufficiently defined in terms of explicitly identifiable neurochemical processes); the weaker position hold to the perceptual ontology (what each individual sees, feels, and thinks contributes to the construction of reality).

Where does all this leave us with regard to materialism? For one thing, we can probably all admit that we are physical beings that are affected by neurophysical and neurochemical process. For another thing, though, there are aspects of belief, emotion, thought, etc. that are not explained by neuroscience. Belief that science will eventually provide all of the answers is just that—belief. For example, the materialists claim that mental states are, in fact, nothing more than brain states has not been proved. The strong materialist reduction to brain states has implications for education and learning. The processes of learning—including memory and understanding—would depend on manipulation of neural processes to achieve desired effects. The simplest version of such materialism is behaviorism; not only have we disposed of behaviorism as a viable educational stratagem, so too have psychologists. That said, at this time psychology does suggest many sound foundations for the ways people learn and the processes individuals go through when confronted by something new. These are exciting developments; before exploring some of them, we should take a look at some less radically materialist ideas.

Brain and Mind

Many psychologists, neuroscientists, and philosophers who suggest alternatives to the strong materialism accept that we are indeed physical beings living in a material world. Understanding consciousness (and belief, learning, knowledge, etc.), for these individuals, is not an intractable problem. John Searle is probably the most forceful alternative thinker, and his counter-arguments to Dennett and others are quite convincing. Yes, I am dismissing the strong materialists; they have little to offer the world of education. Other neuroscientists, such as Walter Freeman (1997), adopt an existentialist point of view towards perception and learning. Freeman maintains that that brain does not constitute the limits of the mind; the body, the environment, and communication with others help to shape how a person learns. He writes that, "The intentional self can be observed by others in society as the seat of action" (p. 113). Freeman is definitely a materialist, but he is open to complex interactions among people and between people and the world around them. The interactions can include representations of the semiotic sort (see Freeman, 2000). From scientists like Freeman we can develop a skepticism (in the sense of questioning) of any simple answers provided by strong materialists.

Searle, Colin McGinn, and others deflate the strong materialist claims effectively and (more importantly) present ways for all of us to reflect on what learning and knowledge are. If one accepts that reflection is a *real* phenomenon, then strong materialism cannot make sense. Searle (1997) expresses his version of materialism thusly: "The brain is indeed a machine; and its processes, such as neuron firings, are organic machine processes. But computation is not a machine process like neuron firing or internal combustion; rather, computation is an abstract mathematical process that exists only relative to conscious observers and interpreters" (p. 17). The conscious observers and interpreters are (among others) teachers, students, and thinkers. Searle (1997) is very effective at dismantling arguments by the likes of Churchland and Dennett. He takes a straw-man syllogism of that represents Churchland's argument:

1. Sam knows his feeling is a pain.
2. Sam does not know that his feeling is a pattern of neuron firings.
3. Therefore Sam's feeling is not a pattern of neuron firings (p. 30).

As Searle points out, Churchland's intellectual opponents are making no such argument. The syllogism begins with an epistemological premise (what Sam *knows*) and ends with an ontological conclusion (what pain *is*). The feeling of pain is qualitative, caused by a physical phenomenon. Imagine seeing your best friend fall and sprain her ankle. You do not feel the qualitative sense of pain that she does, but you may feel a qualitative sympathetic physical sensation, a sensation you may not feel if you read a story about someone falling and spraining an ankle.

Searle also addresses Dennett's position, and his argument in favor of qualitative experience features here also. The subjective sensations or thought, Searle says, are denied by Dennett. Dennett (1991) creates an amusing thought experiment to illustrate his point that qualitative subjective states do not exist. He writes, "Why should a 'zombie's' crushed hopes matter less than a conscious person's crushed hopes?... Postulating special inner qualities that are not only private and intrinsically valuable, but also unconfirmable and uninvestigatable is just obscurantism" (p. 450). Searle (1997) responds, "The reason a zombie's 'crushed hopes' matter less than a conscious person's crushed hopes is that zombies, by definition, have no feelings whatever. Consequently nothing literally matters about their inner feelings, because they do not have any" (p. 108). Human beings, on the other hand, have not only feelings of pain, but also motivation, belief, reflection, questioning, hope, and desire. These qualitative phenomena also carry implications for education. A student can want to learn, be stimulated by ideas, be bored by a presentation, or be confused by a discussion. These are not merely neural states; a confused student may (among other choices) lose interest in a course or may be driven to alleviate the confusion. The subjective state causes the student's actions.

Colin McGinn (1999) chooses not to address Dennett, Churchland, and others directly. Ho does, however, present arguments that call strong materialism into question; he refers to the difficulty of explaining consciousness as "mysterian." Some of the problems he identifies were mentioned in Chapter One. He sums up the problem succinctly: "These two points are entirely obvious: we are aware of consciousness inwardly, while we are aware of the brain outwardly" (p. 47). While his diagnosis seems simple, it carries enormous import. Churchland confuses ontology and epistemology; McGinn clarifies the differences. For each of us our beliefs, thoughts, and customs are our own; they are what we experience and what we can know. Neurochemical functions are real, but we cannot experience and know them as such. We cannot reflect upon them, but we can reflect on why we believe something. McGinn's position is discomforting for anyone who wants to believe in the power of science to provide a full and eliminative explanation of consciousness in physical terms, but it is vital to teaching and learning. Those who would be distressed by what McGinn says are likely to place very strong credence in what is called "epiphenomenalism" (mental states are secondary to, and derived from, physical states). McGinn, in readily admitting the physical foundation of consciousness, hits upon the crux of the disagreement between strong materialists and others—they (both groups) are talking about different things. Consciousness—that is, sentience, perception, smelling, and touching—is bound to our physical selves. *Self*-consciousness is far more difficult to explain. How do we think about how we think? As McGinn (1999) points out, "In the same way, human phenomenology is not reducible to our physiology, since an alien scientist who did not share our senses would not learn our phenomenology just by delving into our brains" (p. 23).

There is, without question, a level of agreement among people studying the brain, the mind, and consciousness. The physical functionality of the brain, in some computational sense, is necessary for the experience of consciousness. But is it sufficient? John Horgan, a science reporter who has a knack for synthesizing complex ideas and adding perceptive conclusions, counts himself among the mysterians. He has broad knowledge of the scientific tradition, the successes of many fields that employ a reductive method in order to define and limit possibilities, and also the disagreements among scientists when confused by the challenges of mind and consciousness. Horgan (1999) writes, "Some mind-scientists, while acknowledging the limitations of all current approaches to the mind, prophesy the coming of a genius who will see patterns and solutions that have eluded all his or her predecessors" (p. 260). The cumulative knowledge in the field of, say, physics still does not lead to successful explanation and prediction of all phenomena (or nearly all, for that matter). Free will, creativity in the plastic and graphic arts, the composition of music, and many other rather commonplace human actions still defy final explanation. For our purposes in understanding learning processes more clearly, we can build upon an invaluable observation that Searle (2007) makes: "[C]onsciousness... is not ontologically reducible to physical microstructures. This is not because it has some extra thing; rather, it is because consciousness has a first-person, or subjective, ontology, and is thus not reducible to anything that has a third-person, or objective, ontology" (p. 50). The first-person ontological perspective is, of course, what is involved in learning and it is further complicated by the phenomenological perspective. Searle is not alone. David Papineau (2003) provides a summary of the stance I believe to be optimal. He frames the summary in two theses:

> First, we should be *ontological monists*. We need to identify conscious properties with material properties, if we are to have a satisfactory account of how conscious causes affect the physical world. Second, we should be *conceptual dualists*. We need to recognize a special phenomenal way of thinking about conscious properties, if we are to dispel the confusions that so readily persuade us that conscious properties cannot be material (p. 175).

Metacognition

Enter metacognition—thinking about thinking. Dennett (1991) does not speak of metacognition (although he includes two brief mentions of meta-knowledge) or self-consciousness at all. A large collection of contributions on cognition (Lycan, 1990) contains 37 pieces; there is no mention of metacognition and only one systems-related mention of self-consciousness. Jerome Kagan (2006), though, suggests a fascinating way to examine the opposition of strong materialists and others (a way that is spoken of by McGinn and Searle, but not quite as eloquently as Kagan). The strong materialists employ a particular vocabulary to frame their questions, state their hypotheses, seek evidence, and articulate theories. It is the language, primarily, of neuroscience (pp. 211-13). In that vocabulary there is little or no place for "meta" or "self." I am arguing for the preference of Searle and McGinn mainly because they are linguistic pluralists. Not only do they accept and use the speech of science, they use the language of phenomenology (as I am using it) and self-consciousness. They are astute enough to know that the speech of neuroscience *cannot* ask questions about metacognition, self-consciousness, and phenomenology. Kagan (2006) offers a useful analogy. If you go to a museum and stand very close to a painting by, say, Monet, you see dollops of textured colors that are variously distinct and intermingled. If you step back you may begin to see lilies in a pond. The neuroscience language is the up-close perception. The language of the likes of Searle, et al., is the language of perception from some distance. There is yet another language; speaking as reminiscent of a Sunday twenty years ago, spent at the museum, spent with the person who would soon become husband or wife.

The need for a clearer understanding of cognitive, including divergent, ideas as mental processes is straightforward—the ways that people think affect the ways they learn. The positions of Searle, McGinn, and others have room for examination of a variety of reactions to the presentation of information, the responses to assignments, and attending to subject matter. The reactions are volitional; they are choices that are made by individuals. The strong materialist does not allow for volition; in practice materialism does not account for the creative assimilation of what is experienced into something new. Specifically, teachers need to find ways to work with students so that students gain understanding of abstract ideas and then employ the abstract ideas in their actions. It is precisely in this objective that constructivist learning takes place in some particular manifestations. To repeat a point from earlier, I am not using constructivism in the way that pervades educational theory. George Hein (1991), for example, defines a specific version of cognitive constructivism: 1) we have to focus on the language in thinking about learning (not on the subject/lesson to be taught); 2) there is no knowledge independent of the view attributed to experience (constructed) by the learner, or community of learners (www.exploratorium.edu/IFI/resources/constructivistlearning.html).

Hein's definition is more extreme than others, but most advocates of constructivist theory agree on some versions of the two points. The approach I am arguing for accepts some of the bases of the points, but rejects the extremes. The emphasis in the first point on the learner is well placed. However, a key principle of phenomenology is that knowledge (or experience) is knowledge (or experience) *of something*. That is, knowledge is not completely abstract; it has an object. It is not only impractical, it is impossible to teach without teaching some subject matter or content. Only a melding of the learner's outcomes and the content of what is learned is meaningful. The second point of Hein's echoes von Glasersfeld's (1995) contention that was critiqued in the first chapter. The aforementioned description of social epistemology is the response to the problematic aspect of constructed knowledge. As is the case with Hein's first point, the construction of knowledge entails construction *of something, from something.* Social epistemology is normative; constructivism is non-normative. In short, without norms constructivism, in its extreme form, is a theory about neither knowledge nor learning. If an objective for librarians is to enable students to evaluate sources and materials, the evaluation will have criteria that allow qualitative distinctions to be made. Evaluation is not possible without some norms.

The kind of construction I am speaking of owes a debt to Kant (1990 [1781]). He said that people inevitably see the world through categorizing eyes. We have concepts that we apply to our perceptions, so when we see a large geological structure looming ahead of us we think "mountain." The conceptualization of perception goes even further, though; mountains also signify things—skiing, climbing and hiking, the geology itself, memories of family vacations, mythology, etc. In other words, our senses are not blind; senses and thoughts converge. We cannot have one without the other. Robert Fogelin (2003) helps us understand what Kant was getting at: "the world as we apprehend it is shaped or organized by mind-imposed concepts or categories. The world as it appears to us is not a pure deliverance of the senses but is instead the joint product of what the sense give us and what the mind imposes… For Kant, perception that is not structured by thought is blind, that is, incapable of serving as the basis for knowledge (p. 71). So construction is not purely social either.

As people learn in formal settings there is usually complex interaction going on. Even in a straightforward lecture the attentive student is listening and also questioning. The student may be trying to fill in gaps in a lecture (apart from formal "informational" gaps). Questions such as, why was there a particular outcome to a sequence of events, what was the effect on people's lives, or did that action cause the response, are some of the thoughts that might run through a student's mind. In a more dialogic setting the instruction can be overtly intentional. It is not unusual for a teacher to ask a question in order to get a predetermined answer. Imagine a classroom where a teacher asks students a question so that everyone can seek an answer. The first, predetermined, sort of questioning is necessary as an ongoing evaluative tool, but the second is based on a different kind of cognitive action. In the first instance an information-processing model can offer suggestions for the retrieval activity of the student. Even if materialists are correct, in the second instance a more complicated process is underway. The second event is one of a different order of consciousness; it involves creation, not merely retrieval (and it entails "listening-rhetoric").

Something even more mysterious can be taking place during dialogic and exploratory discourse in the classroom. It is something that, so far, has escaped elimination. The mysterious complex has a number of elements and requires that each of us examine the customarily unexamined. An element of the phenomenological classroom is that elusive idea that I mentioned earlier—metacognition. The very act of learning entails internal cognitive actions but, at least as importantly, a subjective awareness of others who have things to say, write, and show. There are material reasons for the subjectivity: each person has a unique familial experience; each person has a particular educational background; every individual has a distinct brain and neurophysical system. The things each of us brings to the table will be related, but not identical. The relatedness is consequent to the experiential and physical characteristics. For example, if a person has experienced a natural disaster first-hand, the person's understanding of the event will be different from that of a person who has seen the disaster televised after (or even during) the fact. That is a fairly crude example; more subtle phenomena affect learning. Suppose a student's father and mother are electrical engineers. The parents may have imparted background to their child, the student. That student may be more advanced than others in mathematics, circuitry, and other areas. Conversely, many students will be presented in classes with subject matter that they have never come across. Their subjective experiences will likely be marked by initial confusion. When we use the phrase "steep learning curve" we are instinctively describing the kind of experience the students are going through. Moreover, the presentation of new subject matter will be experienced psychologically by students. Subjective responses, including confusion, anxiety, anger, or excitement, will differ from student to student.

In phenomenological cognitive action the experience of learning does not stop with the subjective. While it is true that each individual is indeed unique, each individual is not solitary. The power of the kind of constructivist learning environment that I am advocating is that it avoids the problem of atomism. Atomism refers to the presumption that "individual" is all there is; that is, each person's experiences, thoughts, and actions are untouched by living with others. In phenomenological terms, our experiences, while not entirely social, are to a considerable extent intersubjective. We live with others, and our Being is affected by what others do and, especially, say to us. The genuine objective of collaborative learning is the emphasis on the intersubjective. A practical outcome of interaction that not only allows for problem solving by groups, but by the metacognitive articulation of the problem-solving process, is reducing the psychological state of being behind, left out, or somehow deficient. When it becomes apparent to a student that he is not as advanced as another in mathematics, and that other student has parents who are engineers, the difference becomes much clearer to the first student. Simple questions asked among students, such as "how did you know that," can facilitate learning. What is exchanged is not merely data, but connections of thoughts. The act of making such connections is a vital metacognitive tactic that is not innate.

In order to learn most effectively the teacher and the students must become aware of their thinking. Each individual has to investigate thought (in the abstract) and thoughts (in a much more concrete way). Here is an example: The instructor in a library's programs speaks to the class about framing questions. A very simple example is a data-based question, such as the most recent trend of mortgage interest rates, the record of the college's football team, or the measures of the world's climate. The class can explore such matters as explicitly "what" questions; the framing of the question may begin, "what is..." A related set of questions might follow, such as how one might take advantage of mortgage interest rates—the class can examine this type of "how" question, which has a different origin than does a "what" question, and is framed differently. The "what" question may be a component of an assignment in another class; the origin is the instructor of that class, and the framing is in the form of eliciting accurate data so as to complete the assignment successfully. The "how" question may have its origin in the inquirer herself; she wants to pay the least possible interest on a house over time, thus enabling her to have access to more money for a variety of purposes. Suppose we add a "why" question; why do mortgage interest rates fluctuate in particular ways over time? Again, the origin may be internal to an individual; he is a financial planner who wants to have a "thick" understanding of the causes of the fluctuations so as to advise clients most effectively.

It is almost impossible to overstate the importance of framing questions. Consider the student who attempts to complete a teacher's assignment when the student has, at best, incomplete understanding of the assignment. The student may be able to apply some mechanisms by which a response can be offered (for example, that student may be able to provide evidence of a search for information in a teacher-recommended database). What is missing is the articulation of a clear question that suggests, or points to, possibilities for answers. Without awareness of the possibilities there may remain only the mechanics. The effort may be rewarded by the teacher, but the substance of the assignment is not addressed by the student. The problem in this example is two-fold: (1) the teacher is somewhat at a loss to evaluate the student's performance, since the student did not actually accomplish the objectives of the assignment, and (2) the student is somewhat at a loss to reflect on what might have been learned by successful completion of the assignment. The information-retrieval cart is before the learning horse. As a result, the intentionality of the assignment and the student's performance gets lost. There is no full comprehension of the "matter" of the assignment.

Hamlet, Act II, Scene 2

Polonius: What do you read, my lord?

> **Hamlet:** Words, words, words.
> **Polonius:** What is the matter, my lord?
> **Hamlet:** Between who?
> **Polonius:** I mean the matter you read, my lord.

Hamlet is being obscurantist on purpose, but the student is likely to be more like Polonius in the misunderstanding of the gist of the conversation/assignment. In a situation where the student understands the nature of the assignment and the intended outcome, something akin to Searle's (2002) observation holds: "The intrinsic intentionality of the agent is doing all the work. To see this point notice that the psychological explanation of my doing long division is not the algorithm, but my *mastery* of the algorithm and my *intentionally* going through the steps of the algorithm" (p. 123).

There is now some empirical inquiry that addresses the difficulties just described. Alison Head and Michael Eisenberg (2009) interviewed a number of students at a variety of institutions and find that context may be missing as the students begin to work on assignments. The students may not be aware of the "big picture" in which the assignment is located, or they may not have facility with the technical language of the field in question, or they may not fully comprehend the parameters of the assignment.

Outcome of Metacognition

It would do no good to speak of metacognition if it did not contribute something to learning. The literature of education addresses this issue. In one instance, Marcantonio Spada and colleagues (2006) find that metacognitive skills can alleviate test anxiety in students. Also, Frans Prins and his co-authors (2006) discover that metacognitive analysis is very beneficial when learners are operating at the boundaries of their knowledge bases (in other word, thinking about thinking helps students comprehend the unfamiliar more readily). Research does tend to demonstrate that metacognitive skills enhance learning ability. Let us take as a given that lower-level undergraduate students are facing a lot that is new to them—subject matter that is more advanced and/or different from their high school experiences, demands that may be greater than they were in high school, and a support system that is less well structured than they are accustomed to (autonomous classes with different groups of fellow students, less frequent contact with teachers, etc). In short, there is an expectation on the parts of many colleges and universities, explicit or tacit, that students are independent learners. If the apparatus for some degree of independence is not acquired in high school, the students may be at a disadvantage in college. Assumptions may be made by their teachers and the assumptions may be lacking substantive foundation. Libraries' instructional programs, and the instructors in the programs, should not fall prey to these kinds of assumptions.

Hilary Putnam (2002) writes, "it is much easier to say, 'that is a value judgment,' meaning, 'that's just a matter of subjective preference,' than to do what Socrates tried to teach us: to examine who we are and what our deepest convictions are and hold those convictions up to the searching test of reflective examination" (p. 44). I quote Putnam here because there is no way I could have communicated the idea better. Students who do not reflect may be able to express personal preferences that are unencumbered by reason or background. If expression is the sole objective of a course of study, then there is no need whatsoever for any evaluative analysis of what others say, write, and show. The ACRL Standards and the writings on information literacy imply that there is more to instruction than mere expression. The questioning challenge arises again. The "what," "how," and "why" questions that teachers impose upon students are attempts to achieve Putnam's goal. I could believe that the earth is (geophysically) flat, but there is no way that I could state, "The earth is flat" without admitting that this is what I want to believe, despite all evidence to the contrary. While belief in a flat earth is an absurd thought, more subtle and more immediate things are the matters of belief by college students. Scientific, political, economic, and other issues are potential areas for belief formation by students. An ostensible reason for the students' presence at the college or university is to develop beliefs that are both substantive and reasoned.

Rationality and Reasoning

Introduction of rationality is important here. [I am not referring to school of thought called rationalism, which had its beginnings in the seventeenth century. That school of thought prized formal logic and observation above subjective reasoning.] Not all cognition is rational. Many things can get in the way of reasoning, including physiological factors. Also, much of cognition entails some processing that is based on emotion and other elements. In his excellent popular work, *How We Decide*, Jonah Lehrer (2009) explains that "human emotions are rooted in the predictions of highly flexible brain cells, which are constantly adjusting their connections to reflect reality. Every time you make a mistake or encounter something new, your brain cells are busy changing themselves. Our emotions are deeply empirical" (p. 41). It appears that even emotion is a kind of rationality. Education depends on the development and exercise of rational processes. So far, so good. But "rational" can still apply to many things. Claude Shannon's (1949) mathematical theory of communication, for instance, is rational. As an engineer, Shannon identified a problem of message transmission over discrete channels. The task at hand for him was to apply engineering principles to develop high-fidelity transmission and receipt of messages. He said repeatedly that semantics—meaning—had little or nothing to do with the problem as he identified and attacked it. Shannon applied rational means both to identify the problem and to search for a solution to it. Those rational means do not help anyone who is trying to discern the meaning of a message. Other rational means would have to be applied to interpretation of the message. Fred Dretske (1981) points out that mathematical theories that compute aggregates, means, and other such properties of transmission cannot be applied to particular messages and especially the content of those messages (p. 48). So, as Dretske, says, misinformation or disinformation are not species of the genus "information;" they are different things altogether. The simplest way to make the distinction that Shannon and Dretske are making is to say that mathematical reasoning and linguistic reasoning are not identical.

Mathematical reasoning is essential, but it is not the primary focus here. Becoming informed (assessing what others say, write, and show) depends more on linguistic reasoning. I am using "linguistic" in a broad sense here, including the semantic along with the syntactical and grammatical. Carol Kuhlthau (2004), who is cited frequently in the information literacy literature, speaks of making sense or meaning out of information. What people tend to do, that is, is seek meaning. I do not dispute her principal concern, but the act of seeking meaning is nonlinear and is complex. "Rational" does mean only application of the strict laws of logic; it also means subjecting thoughts, ideas, claims, and propositions to some criteria of judgment. The cognitive act of becoming informed requires more than seeking meaning in Kuhlthau's terms. It requires identifying and weighing reasons. In part this entails asking "why" questions of what others say, write, and show. Moreover, it entails recognizing that some reasons are "better" than others. A rational reason-giving usually includes assertion of preference, such as, "I'd rather believe A than B." In fact, that kind of preference is not a reason. In logical terms, a reason should be both valid and true.

Here another cognitive challenge is introduced. Suppose we take the following syllogism as an example:

> All librarians are left-handed;
> Albert is a librarian;
> ☐ Albert is left-handed.

This is a valid argument; the conclusion follows logically from the premises. The first premise, though, can easily be disproved; it is an empirical matter. "Valid" does not mean "true" even though there is a rational progression to the syllogism. Now consider the next syllogism:

> All unmarried men are bachelors;
> Albert is an unmarried man;
> ☐ Albert is a bachelor.

This syllogism is logically valid and, according to lexical characteristics of the English language, it is also true (if, and only if, Albert is indeed an unmarried man). These phenomena refer less to how cognition *does* work and more to how cognition *can/should* work. In a college course a student should not merely seek meaning, but should seek some sort of verifiable meaning. Borrowing from Putnam, the responsibility of students is to seek *external* reasons for beliefs about the subject matter of courses. This means that a student should look for evidence outside herself or himself (her or his preferences) to affirm or disaffirm statements. Libraries' instructional programs are loci of learning about the efficacy of external reasons. Again, evaluation is based in just such external reasons.

The cognitive challenge just outlined manifests itself in some particular ways in instructional programs. A component of any course or session is the demonstration of information sources, such as databases.

The procedures for searching are likely to be covered in class, but so too is the assessment of retrieved items. An intentional element of the course or session may be deliberately to introduce students to conflicting statements. The instructor may then ask students what they will do with the conflicting items. The non-reflective response of a student would be to select which item he or she prefers (without subjecting the preference to any testing). A more reflective response would be to delve into the matters of conflict. Students can, individually or collectively, scrutinize each item to find the logic of the claims, the evidence presented, possible evidence that is omitted, etc. The item selected is likely to be the one that survives the challenges of questioning. Students may enter a course thinking that the items in an academic database will be equally authoritative; librarians and faculty know that this is not the case. Since the occurrence in an academic database is not sufficient evidence to believe the claims of any given item, other rational means of assessment have to be applied. I am arguing in this book that the cognitive/evaluative apparatus of students must begin to be developed in libraries' instructional programs.

A primary element of the cognitive assessment of claims is the realization that conflict and inconsistency, while demonstrating potential errors, are not indicators that reason cannot be applied to the matter in question. Donald Davidson (2001) clarifies this point: "Inconsistency, or other forms of irrationality, can occur only within the space of reasons; inconsistencies are perturbations of rationality, not mere absence of rationality" (p. 125). This is probably a difficult concept for undergraduate students to grasp. Perhaps the most effective tool to introduce in class is the outrageous claim. Controversial examples exist; Holocaust denial is one such example. The denial still attempts to offer reasons for the belief. Deniers may state that demographics suggest only a small number of people died, or that the gas chambers would not have been able to handle the volume, or that Germany would not have done such a thing. The deniers would still be couching their claims in the realm of rationality, although they would have to ignore overwhelming evidence that is contrary to what they say. Educational programs of all types, at all levels, must teach the resolution of conflict and of inconsistency. No claim should be accepted or denied without reason being applied. Reasoning is, as Wayne Booth (2004) says, a way to reach the truth about some matter.

Climate change is another issue that has been in the news and has been the subject of dispute. As an example related to reasoning, we can take the work of one researcher, Michael Mann, has received attention by politicians. Mann's articles present longitudinal analyses of temperature patterns dating back several centuries. According to his work, the most recent century has seen a temperature rise that is higher than at any time in the period of analysis. U.S. Representative Joe Barton (R, Texas), Chair of the House Committee on Energy and Commerce convened hearings to hear evidence on Mann's research findings. His Committee commissioned three statisticians to conduct an examination of Mann's work; that panel reported discovering some statistical problems with Mann's analysis. The panel of statisticians had no expertise in paleoclimatology, though. Two other statisticians, Stephen McIntyre and Ross McKitrick, published some papers criticizing Mann and his colleagues as well, and their testimony was also admitted by the Committee. Other scientists who testified, however, affirmed the validity of the body of Mann's work. The norms that generally inform the evaluation of scientific work were bypassed by a political process that sought to discredit Mann and his colleagues and to deflate climate change research findings. One thing that was ignored is the fact that Mann's articles have been cited favorably by a large majority of citing researchers; many of the citing researchers used Mann's methods and their work resulted in very similar findings. This example is presented here to illustrate the complex social and political factors that can affect how people may think about specific areas of research (see Budd, 2007 for an analysis of the above events).

The actions of the House Committee demonstrate that rationality can indeed be perverted, and that it can be perverted by seemingly rational subjects and processes. Evaluation according to the ACRL Standards would have students look for the authority of the speaker. A U.S. Representative, in combination with a panel of academics, might appear to have authority in a matter such as the public policy implications of climate change research. Engaging in clear and critical thinking necessitates a somewhat different standard for authority. The position of the speaker is indeed one criterion; someone who has conducted research in the area in question may have a deeper perspective than a lay person would. If the results are published in a peer-reviewed journal, the nature of the review process might be another criterion. Citations to the published work could be yet another criterion. A standard, expressed as these criteria, is procedural; it accounts only for the nominal elements of authority. Granted, undergraduate students may not be able to move beyond these nominal elements, but they should be introduced to the existence of substantive elements so that they can become accustomed to richer evaluation once they begin course work in their major subjects. When the students become familiar with methods of inquiry in their majors, they will be expected to assess work according to the more substantive criteria of method.

Clear Thinking and Choice

One of the cognitive challenges that every human being faces throughout a lifetime is the conundrum of choice. This challenge is a key part of any instructional program or session. Searches for what people say, write, and show may well yield many items. Are some of the items better than others? How can one tell which are better? What does one do when faced with overwhelming possibilities? ("Better" is defined here according to the evaluative criteria discussed here, including those in the ACRL Standards.) Barry Schwartz (2004) has studied the phenomenon of choice, especially choice among many alternatives. He concludes that some guiding principles, while seemingly counterintuitive, provide the most effective means for approaching choice in an environment of abundance:

1. We would be better off if we embraced certain voluntary constraints on our freedom of choice, instead of rebelling against them.
2. We would be better off seeking what was "good enough" instead of seeking the best (have you ever heard a parent say, "I only want what's 'good enough' for my kids"?)
3. We would be better off if we lowered our expectations about the results of decisions.
4. We would be better off if the decisions we made were nonreversible.
5. We would be better off if we paid less attention to what others around us were doing? (p. 5)

Schwartz's suggestions owe a considerable debt to thought of Herbert Simon, Nobel laureate in economics. As has been noted, Simon coined the word, "satisfice" to represent solutions or outcomes that are good enough. Quite a bit of Simon's attention was on playing games (especially as it tends to model economic decision making). Strategies and tactics that are sufficient to win the game are likely to produce the most consistently positive results.

The messages of Schwartz and Simon are particularly relevant to the content of libraries' instructional programs (even though there are some problematic aspects of satisficing). To illustrate the point of satisficing from a different of view, there is the case of a faculty member who is trying to write the definitive study of a particular subject. For that person, nothing less than certainty will do; the faculty member must examine all possible sources and must evaluate each as thoroughly as possible. Satisficing, for the faculty member, means completeness of search and assessment. The typical undergraduate student is in quite a different position. For one thing, assignments for the undergraduate are frequent and have short turn-around times. Thoroughness is not really a viable option. What is needed is a set of secondary works that address the key elements of the assignments and genuinely inform (give shape to) the student's thoughts. In order to manage time and the assignments originating in several courses, the student will have to comprehend the complexity of the environment. The complexity is characterized by numerous tasks, tasks of differing kinds, tasks of different weightings (e.g., worth varying points towards a final grade), and individual motivation. The complexity can also be heightened by the absence of context (Head and Eisenberg, 2009). The factors are (usually tacitly) balanced, and the actions taken towards accomplishment of the tasks are apportioned according to the balance. At least, in ideal situations students will behave this way. At the beginnings of their college lives students may well be unaware that the balancing is necessary; they may never have had to manage complexity to such an extent. Becoming aware of, thinking about, the challenge of balancing may itself be a learning outcome in a libraries' instruction program or instruction session in a course. Such an outcome is more substantive than many in the ACRL Standards.

Herbert Simon emphasizes that satisficing is actually an exercise of rationality. People (in all walks and stages of life) are faced with complex problem-solving events; effective action requires apportioning attention and effort in ways that will lead to solutions that are good enough. The perfect solution might take so long and require so many resources that it is untenable; also, seeking the perfect solution to one problem may require ignoring other problems. Effective problem solving rests on some sophisticated cognitive strategies. To reiterate an essential point, the first cognitive step is to frame the question. An axiom in carpentry is, "Measure twice; cut once." The lesson of the axiom is that careful work on the front end of a project can result in the most efficient use of time and effort. Following from that beginning, understanding of the optimal process for problem solving enhances efficiency. Here we have metacognition epitomized. Skill with the specific aspects of the process is necessary, but not sufficient. Students need to know why the process is the way it is, why there is a first step, and why the process is usually successful. Metacognitive action is a roadmap to choosing wisely.

How Do We Know What's Good Enough?

This may be the $64,000 question. The answer actually is variable; the more one knows, the less easy it is to tell, in some ways, if one is getting good enough information. The reason for the difficulty may be counter-intuitive. When one has little awareness of the intricacies of a particular topic, every bit that is introduced is likely to have a substantial impact on one's consciousness. For instance, if I know next to nothing baking, becoming aware of the necessity to measure ingredients carefully is very important. The more I know about baking, the more I can focus on the subtleties of introducing new ingredients through experimentation. Here the distance between students and teachers may be most profound. An imperative for teachers, as I mentioned earlier, is imagining not knowing something. Of course that is next to impossible, but the students do not have either the accumulation of information or the body of knowledge that the teacher has. This means that poorer teachers may presume too much; they may think that students know more than they can possibly know. So, throwing things like call numbers, database fields, and sources of data at students will probably have little or no impact. Treating something like a call number as a kind of code gives students something of a context in which to put the call number. Students may be vaguely aware that call numbers are addresses for books and other materials. Do instructors have reason to believe that the students would know that call numbers indicate something more? A perceptive student may have discovered that the book she was looking for is near other books on similar subjects. If that student has other such experiences, she may begin to look in the vicinity of a particular book for more on the subject.

Students may not discern that classification systems are just that. They are intentional structures designed to order things. As students search a library's catalog they may become aware of the usefulness of subject headings. The subject headings are words that will look familiar; they are names that can be applied to things. There is, however, no reason to take for granted that students will intuit the intentionality that has gone into the creation and use of the classification structures. In actuality, classification is complex; it is an action by humans to infer or impose order on something. In the case of books, journal articles, Web sites, and other packages, the creators intended to convey meaning. Someone coming along after these things have been created attempt to infer the meaning from the messages included in the package. The act of classifying is simultaneously indicative (it demonstrates the process of inferring meaning *and* the inferred meaning) and misleading. Some cognitive analysis is needed to understand that the classification is contingent. By "contingent" I mean that it is quite probably one person's inference at one point in time, based on less than complete examination of the content. When it comes to things like journal articles the contingency may be less severe; the content is briefer and may be constrained by the nature of the package. A journal, say *College & Research Libraries*, has content that is limited to a topic and an environment. A classifier (indexer) already knows that the subject of an article will have boundaries. The classifier can then pay attention to more specific attributes of the article.

At this point it is useful to revisit an earlier notion. John Searle (2001) writes about the nature of rationality and how it actually works. When it comes to classifying what people say, write, and show, the classifier has to apply some sort of direction of fit. Specifically, the classifier applies a "mind-to-world" fit: "It is the task of the belief, as part of the mind, to represent or fit an independently existing reality, and it will succeed or fail depending on whether or not the content of the belief in the mind actually does fit the reality in the world" (Searle, 2001, p. 37). The fit is not perfect; the classifier is not describing a rock or a subatomic particle. The classifier holds belief of "aboutness" applied to another belief of sorts. That is, one person is inferring meaning about a text created by another person—a text that someone attempted to imbue with intended meaning. There will be some gap between the inferred meaning of the classifier and the intended meaning of the creator. In the case of literature, the gap itself may be intentional; an author may want different readers to infer different meanings (or the same reader inferring different meanings at different times). With other texts the gap may be a problem. Searle (2001) goes on at some length to illustrate that the gap is, to a considerable extent, inevitable. Suppose you write an article for a particular journal. You are creating something that is real; the text exists in a tangible/linguistic/logical form. In short, it is ontologically real. However, you created the text from a first-person ontology; it is real from your point of view. You defined the topic; you purposely designed the content; you chose the words. Once the article is published, every reader will see it from varying first-person ontologies. Each reader brings a perspective, a background, to the article.

The example of the article points to a phenomenon of the classroom (physical or virtual). The teacher speaks from a first-person ontology, and every student hears from a first-person ontology. Some philosophers call this the problem of other minds. One camp of the philosophers thinks that this problem cannot be solved; subjectivity amounts to something like an absolute. It is apparent that a phenomenological stance rejects that camp's assertion. Intersubjectivity is possible, even necessary, for all forms of human communication. The thoughts of others are certainly not completely objective (even to the thinker), but there is a strong possibility that the phenomena that are perceived by one person are likely to be observed in similar ways by other observers. Such a realization allows us to know things because of testimony. That said, the problem of other minds does render complete understanding of what others say, write, and show difficult. For the purposes of designing and offering a course or session, the problem may be most evident when helping students comprehend such things as ideological standpoints. When a speaker is not forthright—when that person lies, hides information, twists data, or removes things from their original context—it can be very difficult to infer the full intention of the speaker. There is no guarantee that authors of journal articles or books, or creators of Web sites, will always be honest and open. A particular form of the problem arises when scientists fabricate or falsify data, and report it as valid. The recent case of Hwang Woo Suk, a South Korean researcher, illustrates the point. Suk fabricated data on stem cells and published falsified conclusions that made the research appear to be groundbreaking (see, for example, http://www.pittsburghlive.com/x/pittsburghtrib/s_404170. html). No field of study is free from deliberate misinforming.

Clear Thinking in the Classroom

"Critical thinking," as we've seen, can be somewhat elusive in that there are many definitions and applications of the term. It is possible, though, to pare down some of the opinions. For instance, educational researchers Deanna Kuhn and David Dean (2004) consolidate the possible elements of critical thinking into inquiry and argument: "A cornerstone of inquiry is the idea of a thesis, or question, and potential evidence that bears on it. There must be something to find out" (p. 269). In their investigation of argument Kuhn and Dean find that there is a developmental gap between addressing the claims of others and try-ing only to support one's own claim. The gap presents a teaching and learning opportunity. The inquiry and argument goals that Kuhn and Dean identify are repeated, although not in such a straightforward way, in the education literature. Rebecca Albitz (2007) rightly includes librarians in the process of teaching critical thinking—rightly because librarians are integral to inculcating questioning into students' lives (through instruction in all forms and through the many services offered by libraries). Argument, however, is less widely recognized in the library literature and the Standards as a key component of critical thinking. The judgments that enable evaluation are frequently connected to argument and rhetoric, though. Whether conclusions are warranted on the basis of propositions or evidence is a necessary component of evaluation (see Toulmin, 1958). An instructional program, in order to embrace the entirety of critical thinking, must include argument.

All this discussion of cognitive and thinking about thinking results in a conclusion that should be inescapable—instructors should instill in students a modicum of skepticism. Students, as critical thinkers (which really means applying logic, empirical analysis, common sense, and all cognitive tools available), should learn not to take things at face value. While some phenomena exhibit regularities and can be analyzed by fairly simple means, many (maybe most) are complex and are not matters of central tendency. "Central tendency" is a statistical term that signifies taking a single measure (usually the mean, median, or mode) as representative of the entire population. Some characteristics, such as height, weight, IQ, or test scores, can be simply described, especially when the sample sizes are large. If you were to invite 1,000 people from your town or city (randomly selected from the telephone directory) to show up at a local stadium or arena, you would find that the average height of the group would indeed be close to the height of almost every one of the 1,000 people. If you invited those 1,000 people to the stadium, and also invited Bill Gates, and then measured the wealth or assets of each member of the group, you would arrive at an average that would not be representative of the members of the group. Suppose we assume that the mean net worth of the original 1,000 people is $200,000, and the net worth of Bill Gates is $50,000,000,000. Taking all of the values, the mean for the 1,001 people would be $50,149,850. That figure tells you nothing at all about the vast majority of the people in the group. Much of aggregate analysis (such as calculating mean and median values and scores) may be insensitive to individual instances that skew results. In other words, there may be some systemic conventions that obscure nuances; it is here that reasoning must be applied. In fact, such reasoning illustrates critical thinking as critique.

In fact, an example such as the one just described could be used in class. Anyone could do the arithmetic to derive the mean net worth, but intuition might well lead students to believe that the introduction of Bill Gates into the mix would have a small effect. The skepticism that students should leave the course with can help them combat the intuitions that might result in false conclusions. A similar cognitive strategy applies to matters directly related to libraries' instructional programs. We have seen that classification can be a substantial help to students looking for materials on particular topics. Those classifications or categories are not pure ontologies, though. What I mean by this is that a subject heading, a descriptor, or a call number is an imperfect representation of the content of what people say, write, and show. Nassim Nicholas Taleb (2007) warns that, "Categorizing is necessary for humans, but it becomes pathological when the category is seen as definitive, preventing people from considering the fuzziness of boundaries, let alone revising their categories" (p. 15). I happened upon Taleb's book on display at a local bookstore; I was not familiar with it before I picked it up to browse through it. I found, only by subjecting it to some scrutiny, that I could use it (not merely for this chapter, but to help with crystallizing some thoughts about human cognition). He manages to address some of the complicated issues discussed here with clarify and wit. The subject headings listed in the Cataloging in Publication (CIP) data for the book are "Uncertainty (Information theory)—Social aspects" and "Forecasting." I would guess that those headings would not lead me to the book if, as a physical object, it were placed in a large collection. The skepticism that students leave the course with can help open their minds to possibilities, especially given that, in the abstract, all that exist are possibilities.

KEY POINTS IN CHAPTER FOUR:

➢   Strong materialism or eliminativism are influential in many fields, but they limit the ways we can conceive of learning

➢   Humans *are* material beings, but we examine ourselves by way of the first person; we cannot get outside our consciousnesses

➢   Metacognition, thinking about thinking, offers a deeper first-person examination that every person can use to analyze how we make decisions, assess evidence, and learn

➢   Reasoning, which is related to metacognition, can connect internal and external sources of thought, ideas, evidence, and logic

➢   Critical thinking enables everyone, including students, to make choices, especially of "critical" is taken to mean "critique."

CHAPTER FIVE

◆

A Vision for Learning

There is no doubt that libraries' instructional programs are important. They can become even more vital to the missions of colleges and universities, though. The foregoing chapters have attempted to critique instruction as a way to energize thought and discourse on what could be an essential service. The recommendation throughout this book has been a turn to phenomenological cognitive action. The recommendation has been described, but more can be said about it and the contributions it can make to student learning and student success. Phenomenological cognitive action is, quite frankly, the missing element, not only in libraries' instruction, but in instruction across campuses. That is a very bold statement that needs a considerable amount of support.

Every institution, every college and university, has student learning as a goal. In some institutions, such as community colleges, the learning is intended to have a practical purpose much of the time. Still, the students must learn in order to succeed; they must develop the capability to seek and find what is new, the wherewithal to integrate the new into what they know, and the understanding needed to assess that information that comprises the new. Students at all colleges and universities must similarly gain the ability to explore and evaluate. These abilities are not restricted to information resources; they are at the heart of the phenomenon of learning. They do not constitute skills or competencies in any narrow sense. The abilities become, when they are most effective, part of people's being. As such, the abilities are not limited to the absorption of facts or the accumulation of data. For example, there is a huge difference between history and chronology. An individual may have an awareness of things that happened in, say, 1066 or 1863. Such awareness is touted by, among others, E. D. Hirsch (in his book *Cultural Literacy*). The awareness of chronology is useful to historical examination, but it is not history. Without delving into who was involved in events, what else was occurring in the world, and possible reasons underlying human action, there is no study of history. The difference between chronology and history is that of awareness and understanding. The study of history, as is the case with the study of every subject, encompasses a quest for truth.

In previous chapters the "cognitive" and "action" elements of phenomenological cognitive action have been described, and are likely to be readily comprehensible even without the description. Phenomenology, however, is very complex and deserves more attention. The acknowledged "father" of phenomenology in the sense that I am using it here is Edmund Husserl (1859-1938). His work was original; he approached many issues in ways that no one had previously. After studying mathematics and logic he expanded his work into metaphysics and the ways people experience the world around them. His phenomenological project was continued—and altered—by followers, including Martin Heidegger, Maurice Merleau-Ponty, and Paul Ricoeur. It is primarily Husserl's own work that forms the basis for the recommendation offered here. I am obliged to state that Husserl's writings are very difficult, and my assimilation of them in this chapter constitutes one stage in a continuing effort to grasp them. Far from being the final word, as applied to instruction and beyond, this chapter signals a kind of entrée into Husserl's phenomenology as it can contribute to libraries' instructional programs and education in general. At times I may be able to do little more than ask questions or offer tentative suggestions, but I hope others will add their thoughts to the conversation that this book may foster.

Husserl worked through and tried to refine his thoughts on phenomenology over about four decades, and the refinements are such that one must examine as much of his writing as possible to approach comprehending the complexity. In part, Husserl built upon Descartes's idea of the thinking being—not as a way to affirm Descartes's dualistic separation of mind and body, but to highlight the place of doubt in reflection upon the *ego cogito*—the thinking subject. What Husserl was emphasizing was the need for some degree of initial questioning that would lead to reflection. Reflection would be aimed both at the object of doubt (a heliocentric solar system at one point in time, for instance) *and* the act of doubting. The reflection would be directed at cogitation by the individual thinker (hence, *ego cogito*). To some philosophers the matter stabilizes on the point of reflection itself. For Husserl the emphasis on reflection was nothing more than a starting point, an indispensable beginning on the path to knowledge. Husserl was well aware of the kind of psychological action that characterizes human existence. He had read the writings of William James on psychology, so was familiar with a limitation to perception that James (1950) acknowledged: ""Millions of items of the outward order are present to my senses which never properly enter into my experience. Why? Because they have no interest for me. My experience is what I agree to attend to" (p. 402). What James had to say underscores that attending to things as they seem to be has some fundamental limitations if one stops examination at the moment of perception. Husserl's version of doubt is very important to what I am trying to convey here; we will return to it shortly.

James's observation also hints obliquely at something Husserl tackles directly. While James is correct he does not explore all of the aspects of perception that are there for the taking. The individual perceiver does pay attention to some things and not others, but also the perceiver narrows the gaze that the person exercises intuitively. That is to say, the perceiver, when conscious of something, has directed consciousness at the object. [N.B.: The "object" may be physical and literal, such as another person or a text, or can be non-physical, such as an idea or a memory.] Husserl (2001) himself says, "Perception does not consist in staring blankly at something lodged in consciousness, inserted there by some strange wonder… Rather for every imaginable ego-subject, every objectlike existence with a specific content of sense is an accomplishment of consciousness" (p. 57). One is not merely dimly aware of something; one *sees* another person, one evaluates one's position, one expects a particular event to occur. In many ways, the concept of intentionality is the most important element of phenomenology as it relates to libraries' instructional programs. To believe something is one intentional quality; to know something is a different quality, even if the intentions regard the same object. Dan Zahavi (2003) clarifies: "One is not simply conscious of an object, one is always conscious of an object in a particular way, that is, to be intentionally directed at something is to intend something *as* something" (p. 24).

In the last chapter we saw that students are frequently asked to react to objects (used in the sense detailed above). The reaction can be used to highlight differing intentional qualities. An exercise that presents differing views of intelligent design is one example. When the topic is introduced each student is likely to perceive it in a particular way. One student may believe in intelligent design because of schooling and the personal authority of those who presented a point of view to him. Another may disbelieve it because of parents who introduced a particular scientific viewpoint to her. Those influences may well have helped shape the beliefs that the students hold. They then perceive the opinions and arguments of authors of pieces on the subject. As Husserl affirms, the consciousnesses of the students are not blank when they read the pieces. Because consciousness *is* alive and active the intentional event of reading each piece constitutes an act on the parts of the students, subject to complex cognitive processes. Consciousness is potentially (but not necessarily) affected by every intentional event. The effect of any given even may be small, and may be small because of an absence of reflection. Reflection is by no means autonomic; it must be learned and practiced. The classroom is one place where it can be experienced.

The perceptual actions of the students can, and must, be trained through education, and libraries' instructional programs are excellent places to begin the training. The nature of the kind of thinking required for learning and knowledge is explicated most clearly by Robert Sokolowski in his, *Introduction to Phenomenology* (2000). I commend this book to all instructors for the most succinct yet comprehensive and accessible introductory work on the topic. Sokolowski takes pains to distinguish between two attitudes—the natural and the phenomenological. The natural attitude is more readily intuited and is the commonplace mode of thought in our everyday lives. We comprehend, for example, the heat of fire, the danger of some wild animals, the necessity to follow the rules of the road, and so on. We know these things through experience (direct or indirect), and we appreciate the outcomes related to behaviors that might transgress against common sense. Phenomenologists, including Husserl, demonstrate that the natural attitude is vital to the success of the physical sciences as well. The observation and measurement of physical particles, beings, and events comprise the exactness of these sciences. The natural attitude, then, is nothing to scoff at; it is the fundamental means by which we get through our mundane lives, and is necessary, not only for living, but for moving beyond the experiences that lead us to embrace the natural attitude. We use the natural attitude to understand that what we call water is one atom of oxygen and two of hydrogen. We use the phenomenological attitude to ponder the attribution of life-giving properties to water.

Moving beyond, or transcending, the natural attitude requires adopting a phenomenological attitude. This attitude is needed for philosophical analysis, and entails reflection on the natural attitude. Sokolowski (2000) instructs us: "We contemplate the involvements we have with the world and with things in it, and we contemplate the world in it human involvement" (p. 48). The contemplation is not merely introspection—examination of one's one state, thoughts, and beliefs. It is examination of the world that the self and others live in. I will return to the phenomenological attitude later; at this time it is sufficient to say that it includes critical reflection on *everything*; nothing is taken for granted. The challenges inherent to this aspect of Being are self-evident; colleges students will not come to it easily.

An Aside on the Lives of Freshmen

It is appropriate here to introduce some research that has been conducted on students in their first year of college. The principal reason for inserting the research at this point is that phenomenological cognitive action can be quite demanding on students. It requires some profound changes to people's Being at a time when other profound changes are occurring. Tim Clydesdale (2007) interviewed a number of individuals, first when they were high school seniors, and then when they were freshmen in college. Overwhelmingly, the students' experiences in that first year in college consisted of learning mundane things related to being on their own (laundry, handling money, etc.), adjusting to schedules that are different from the previous year's, confronting new and different relationships with people, and becoming aware of themselves in new ways. The freshmen, Clydesdale found, were not scholars in that first year. They were consumed with changed lives, completely different personal associations, and responsibilities they had not previously had. All this is not to say that freshmen are oblivious to the courses they are taking, but they ten not to be fully engaged in the depth and breadth of learning that others may expect of them. It is possible (perhaps it is more than possible) that teachers are not aware of the magnitude of the changes that freshmen are going through and, more importantly, the psychical effects of the changes on the students.

Clydesdale's analysis of high school seniors and college first year college students is enlightening, particularly as libraries' instructional programs are considered. He (2007) says, "Precious few teens possess a love of learning or a breadth of perspective on the world and their place in it" (p. 157). That said, he notes a pronounced difference in the same people when they have completed that first college year: "Just one year after high school graduation, the difference in teens is obvious. High School seniors who talked in phrases or clipped sentences, as college students now talk in full sentences, even paragraphs. Seniors who stumbled and skipped over more challenging questions, as college students now answer and explain themselves" (p. 167). The first year of college has a string effect on people; it is the responsibility of all in higher education to optimize that impact without overwhelming young people who are undergoing immense change in their lives. We must all remember that people at the traditional age for beginning at college are still developing physically, emotionally, and cognitively. Eighteen-year-olds are likely to be at different stages of development as well. The challenges of working with students who are undergoing such changes are compounded by some apparent gender differences that could have implications for libraries' instructional programs, and first-year course in general. Each year freshmen at U.S. colleges and universities are surveyed, and some of the questions ask individuals to assess themselves in some key areas. Potentially important characteristics where men and women differ include rating themselves in the top 10% in:

Self-confidence (intellectual)	Men – 69.2%	Women – 52.3%
Competitiveness	Men – 70.4	Women – 47.8
Emotional health	Men – 62.1	Women – 48.3
Self-confidence (social)	Men – 58.5	Women – 48.8
Mathematical ability	Men – 53.1	Women – 35.7
Computer skills	Men – 49.3	Women – 32.1

(*Chronicle of Higher Education* 54 (Feb. 1, 2008): A23).

When Clydesdale's findings and the survey results are combined it becomes increasingly clear that libraries' instructional programs must attend to the students as people. It is not an overstatement to assert that too many programs (as critiqued in previous chapters) tacitly treat students as blank slates, ready to absorb sets of skills. Both Clydesdale's work and the survey results suggest that there are vital elements of students' states (emotional and intellectual) that phenomenological cognitive action approach is best suited to address. This approach links, as is evident from the description of possible course content that will be presented in the next chapter, other things the students are experiencing or are already aware of into the cognitive and intellective processes of evaluating what others write, say, and show. The processes are extremely complex and are not reducible to a skill set or cluster of competencies. The phenomenological grounding offered here is a way to build a program that enriches students' complete development.

Back to Phenomenology

In Husserl's last major work he set forth a cogent and compelling argument for a particular path to knowledge and truth. His conception was very much at odds with a tradition that now extends back about four centuries. Beginning with Francis Bacon, method began to eclipse subject and object as the center of scientific (very broadly defined) inquiry. That tradition continued and grew as George Berkeley, John Locke, David Hume, Auguste Comte, and Herbert Spencer solidified method's supremacy. At the time Husserl was writing *The Crisis of the European Sciences* (the later 1930s), logical positivism and behaviorism were powerful forces in both the social and the natural sciences. Husserl (1970) wrote that philosophy "threatens to succumb to skepticism, irrationalism, and mysticism" (p. 3). Just a little further in the book he wrote, "Merely fact-minded sciences make merely fact-minded people" (p. 6). [The critique of information literacy here follows Husserl's warning and also shows the effects of concentration on method. Programs, writings, and standards demonstrate a marked tendency to seek and apply specific methods of pedagogy, profession, and learning. What follows should be read with the foregoing critique in mind, and the end of method's dominance as a goal.]

What Husserl is saying, and I agree enthusiastically with him, is that many people have had an erroneous idea of science, primarily because they have had erroneous ideas of reason, meaning, knowledge, and Being. Unfortunately, the errors are alive and well in much of the academy and in libraries instructional programs. My concerns (stated in previous chapters) regarding information literacy as it exists today center around just these kinds of errors. In part Husserl is criticizing an indefensibly solitary emphasis on objectivity that has found its way into much of the thinking and work in the social sciences at this time. Narrow and constricting objectivity (a denial of subject), among other things, ignores the historical element that permeates all of life and also ignores what Husserl calls the pre-given lifeworld. That lifeworld, which differs substantially from qualitative research definitions of the "lived experiences" of people, embodies the complexities of history—complexities that are both individual and collective. His notions of things like discovery do not abandon method, but they do seek to correct the original errors and to relocate the likes of Descartes (especially) in his phenomenology.

For Husserl, phenomenology is not principally a method, even though what comprises phenomenology can be used to inquire into human action, including learning. For Husserl, the ultimate objective of philosophy and science (in its ancient meaning) is to move past *doxa* (everyday relative knowledge, sometimes referred to as opinion) to *epistēmē* (rational knowledge). Here the roots of phenomenology are very different from the methodological "phenomenology" practiced by many social science researchers. Things like "lived experience" are indeed, in social science inquiry, relative; mine is different from yours. What is missing in this construction is examination of the same pre-given lifeworld that you and I share. So, in Husserl's phenomenology, knowledge, in the strict sense of the word, is possible. That is, not everything we can think about, ponder, discuss, or experiment with, is completely contingent; some things can be known. There are huge pedagogical implications for the difference Husserl asserts.

At this point it may be time to quote a radical statement (made by Maurice Merleau-Ponty (1962)): "phenomenology can be practised [sic] and identified as a manner or style of thinking, that it existed as a movement before arriving at complete awareness of itself as a philosophy" (p. viii). If read quickly and not contemplated, it sounds as though Merleau-Ponty is dismissing phenomenology, but nothing could be farther from the truth. Merleau-Ponty was profoundly influenced by Husserl and, in fact, his statement is an expression of the ontological side of phenomenology. The world is "already there;" it already exists, before we can perceive it (much less reflect upon it). The purpose, the heart, of phenomenology is diametrically opposed to radical constructivism (for instance). Radical constructivism denies ontology; whether or not there is a real world to be perceived is irrelevant, since there are only thoughts about what we think (or imagine) we perceive. Perhaps the most blunt assertion of radical constructivism is that there can be no correspondence theory of truth or knowledge (the idea that truth and knowledge genuinely correspond to what is in the world and how the world is). Phenomenology begins with the premise that correspondences exists, and then builds a way to identify the correspondence. Phenomenology does go further, though; our perceptions are *of* something and our knowledge is *of* something. This reiterates the point made earlier—the natural world and the perceiver (the self) are parts of one reality and cannot be separated from one another.

As part of one reality, the perceiver can indeed perceive the world as it is. Husserl's phenomenology is not a subjective relativism. He (1962) writes, "It is not that the real sensory world is 'recast' or denied, but that an absurd interpretation of the same, which indeed contradicts its *own* mentally clarified meaning, is set aside. It springs from making the world absolute in a *philosophical* sense, which is wholly foreign to the way we naturally look out upon the world" (§ 55, p. 153). Since Husserl was also a mathematician he knew well that there are aspects of reality that, while difficult to grasp fully, simply are. The task for consciousness is to understand, to find meaning in, the world. He said that the finding of meaning in the world is something each of us does every day; as we navigate our way through physical movement, work, interacting with others, and the like, we deal with the world as it is. It is when we are called upon to *find* meaning (not just to apply meanings we have already found or *doxa* with which we are comfortable) that the customary approach to the world becomes a challenge.

How do we face the challenge? More importantly, how do we integrate facing the world into libraries instructional programs? An important part of the answer rests in the way I framed the questions, using "we" instead of "I" or "you." In all of teaching and learning there must be a persistent and pervasive intersubjectivity for there to be success. The intersubjectivity is more than mere awareness and acceptance that someone else os speaking or listening. It is also a deeper understanding that each individual is an *ego cogito*, a thinking and reflecting self, and entails interaction on such a deeper basis. The acceptance of each person as an *ego cogito* carries the responsibility to meet every person as someone who is both learning and knowledgeable. In the classroom the intersubjectivity should be just that—a full comprehension of what "we" comprises. That is, the teacher, in order to help students learn, must forego imparting facts (in the sense of, "Here is a fact that I have; now I am giving it to you). Here we can remember Husserl's admonition about fact-mindedness. The teacher has to retrieve the matter under consideration, must examine it anew and bring the students into that examination, for learning to thrive.

Doubt

There is a means, provided by Husserl, to enact the kind of intersubjectivity just described. His idea is a very complex one, but a somewhat more straightforward version is not only conceivable, but applicable in education. The growth of knowledge for every individual depends on processes of critical reflection. That component is not really new in pedagogy, but the reflection in phenomenology is of a very particular kind. It begins, according to Husserl, with *epochē*, a word which, to the ancient Greeks, meant suspension of judgment. There is a very important thing to realize here: What Husserl is advocating is not the same as the customary philosophical notion of skepticism (something Husserl warns against), or the stance that knowledge and justification are not possible. *Epochē*, as used here, has more in common with the colloquial use of "skepticism," which translates roughly into "doubt." Husserl's *epochē* is a constructive doubt, directed toward the discovery of the meaning of the thing under consideration. It is thus a positive act, since it is open to the possibility that meaning *can* be found. In applying *epochē* in libraries' instructional programs we can introduce students to the act of suspending judgment pending evidence. Evidence, in this process of transcendental *epochē*, is not simply a matter of collecting things like articles, books, or Web sites. The collecting is, perhaps, a necessary act, but it is a means to an end. Evidence is that which is intuitable, can be subjected to reflection. "Any evidence is a grasping of something itself that is, or is this, a grasping in the mode 'it itself', with full certainty of its being, a certainty, a certainty that accordingly excludes every doubt" (Husserl, 1999, p. 15). The definition of evidence shows how libraries' instructional programs must be wary of the limitations of the students; an expectation of complete apprehension of this mode of evidence is likely to meet with some disappointment.

There is something we can take away from Husserl's stricture. In a class, the composition of ontological reality can be presented to students in some concrete ways. For example, a tree can be presumed to be a "whole," an entire entity, to be perceived in its completeness. That whole, though, is comprised of parts, such as limbs, roots, and leaves. A leaf, while a part of the tree, is an independent part (or "piece") of the tree. What this means is that the leaf can be taken on its own, and could actually itself be considered as a whole. Many physical things can be examined according to this pattern of wholes and parts. Other things can be examines in a somewhat different way, even though there are still wholes and parts. Consider a novel, such as Twain's *Huckleberry Finn*. It constitutes a whole, designed and put together by Twain. Its parts are the letters, words, sentences, paragraphs, and chapters. Chapter Three is a part of the novel, but it is a non-independent part; it should be considered only as part of the whole. Likewise "Jim" is a non-independent part. In terms of evidence, anyone considering, say, a position articulated by a political candidate should look at parts— individual statements, premises, propositions, and conclusions. These are parts of the whole position.

Applying *epochē* can enable one to subject the parts and the whole to constructive doubt. The position, as articulated, may be sound, may not be refuted in the process of doubted. Or it may be found wanting. The politician's position can be called a "categorial" object. It is not physical; one cannot touch it or taste it, but it exists. Categorial objects can also be subjected to *epochē*. Perception alone is not sufficient to examine something as complex as a categorial object; study of the properties, or categories, of a things can be extra-perceptual (if perception is limited to sensory perception). In other words, we apply intellection to the examination of the properties. Like sensation, though, this kind of categorization implies ontology, something real. In Husserl's usage of the term, something like a political position or an argument *is* real, in that it can be examined as wholes and parts. Dan Zahavi (2003) summarizes this aspect of phenomenology: "Husserl's concept of experience is far more comprehensive than the one bequeathed to us from empiricism. We not only experience concrete and particular objects, but abstract or universal ones as well" (p. 37).

I have to emphasize that, while we all may be tempted to trivialize that doubt that is part of *epochē* as something we always engage in, Husserl's radical and critical doubt is of a different species, as Zahavi says. It is very difficult to suspend judgment on matters that are familiar or taken for granted, but that is precisely what Husserl and education demand. The radical demand is strict; it is not something that we simply fall into or are drawn to. The reflection that is vital to *epochē* is more than the natural perceptual acts represents by statements such as, "I see a house." Transcendental *epochē* necessitates a different kind of subjectivity—one that is not limited to sensory perception, but extends to a deeper level of Being (Husserl, 1999, § 15, pp. 34-35). It requires, not merely intellectual effort, but a kind of effort that requires us to question what constitutes our Being. Dermot Moran (2005), interpreting Husserl, says that the everyday (natural) doubt that we may engage in is reflection that, "can yield ourselves as subjects, but it does so in the context of an unquestioned, dogmatic commitment to the world, that does not reveal the functioning of the ego in all its constitution," but "is a practice that must be sustained against all temptations to relapse into the natural attitude" (p. 191).

Evaluation

The foregoing presents cause for phenomenology informing libraries' instructional programs. The role that phenomenology can play is strengthened when evaluation of the program is considered. Students will almost inevitably enter college with the natural attitude defining their outlook on everything. As is mentioned above, the natural attitude is necessary; the physical world we live in demands that we are cognizant of basic physical laws. We function on the natural world, so any time we walk, drive, or fly we rely on some awareness of the physical world. A substantial component of learning also relies on the natural attitude. Someone who wants to study, say, mechanical engineering will have to develop a very sophisticated natural attitude. As Sokolowski (2000) says, "The world is the ultimate setting for ourselves and for all the things we experience. The world is the concrete and actual whole for experience," but also, "If the world is the widest whole and the most encompassing context, the I is the center around which the widest whole, with all things in it, is arranged" (p. 44). Simply living in the concrete, natural world is something we do not choose; we can, though, make other choices about our lives. One is to understand the concrete, natural world (or pieces of it) as clearly and deeply as we can. Another is to see understanding and knowledge that is beyond the natural attitude.

The realization of the importance of understanding the natural world appears to shape much of the evaluation that takes place in libraries' instructional programs. It is necessary to examine students on their ability to locate physical materials in a library, to make use of databases as repositories for works on many topics, and to select efficient search mechanisms so as to find works that have topical relation to the searches they conduct. These exercises are as important as learning multiplication tables, long division, diagramming sentences, and other things that are taught as background in schools. The regularities of these kinds of operations do not diminish their essential place in the process of learning. Shikha Sharma (2007) reports on a program at the University of Connecticut, and says that the librarians made the choice to concentrate on some specific skills as part of their course:

1. understanding the cycle and flow of information;
2. developing a research topic using concept mapping;
3. constructing effective search statement;
4. identifying and using appropriate print and online research tools such as the Library's catalog, multidisciplinary and subject-specific databases, and Web resources;
5. understanding all elements of a citation for types of sources; and
6. critically evaluating the quality of print and Web-based information (p. 129).

Numbers 1, 4, and 5 do appear to be developments of students' natural attitudes. The flow of information, for example, is a natural type of process; it is dictated by concerns of production, distribution, access, and preservation. In order to help students learn about those elements the librarians presented possible concept maps to illustrate the attendant factors related to cell phones. The maps (Sharma, 2007, p. 131) demonstrate progressively complex ways to include related factors. The "technological aspects" of cell phones is introduced as a category of concept, then that category is expanded to "history," "system network," and "future trends." The other aspects, especially "health and safety aspects," can be further expanded to demonstrate to kinds of questions that proceed from simpler levels of consideration. This concept mapping can be a very effective pedagogical and evaluative tool that courses everywhere can consider emulating.

The other three elements in the above list also have aspects of the natural attitude, but they require something different, both for success and for evaluation. Sharma (2007) actually notes that "these skills merely serve as tools for realizing [information literacy's] higher goals that include the ability to identify, access, evaluate, and interpret relevant information for making informed decisions" (p. 127). Elements such as the three (numbers 2, 3, and 6) do include some of the natural attitude for the mechanical components of searching and retrieving works, but the phenomenological attitude is needed to seek meaning, both in the act of questioning and in reading what is found. Evaluation of libraries' instructional programs does include some nominal effort at transcending the natural attitude, but too frequently the effort does not recognize that a transcendentally different attitude is needed. Some of the evaluative shortcomings have been exemplified in previous chapters; one more example can serve here. Davida Scharf and colleagues (2007) present the integration of portfolios, along with criteria used to assess the students' portfolios. One criterion is students' demonstration that they have integrated sources so as to interpret, deepen and reflect on topics. This criterion is then mapped to ACRL Standards, Performance Indicators, and Performance Outcomes. Outcomes include: "Recognizes prejudice, deception, or manipulation," and "Integrates new and prior information" (p. 475). The outcomes are admirable, even necessary, but the means for achieving these outcomes are questionable without a conscious shift to a phenomenological attitude, without application of *epochē*. To compound the difficult present in their examination, Scharf, et al. apply natural and mechanistic analyses—a naïve sampling technique, rigid instrumental categories of performance, and a statistical analysis based only on the instrumentalities.

The "attitude" of which I have been speaking has a particular meaning that should be emphasized here, in light of the critique. Matheson Russell (2006) makes the usage clear: "Now, by 'attitude' here is meant an overall manner of being or stance which *orients* our lived experience. In the 'arithmetical attitude', for example, we are oriented towards the world of arithmetical objects. This is our default 'attitude', the one to which we always revert" (p. 59). Russell is showing the power and force of an unquestioned attitude, and that force is evident in the work of Scharf, et al. Even their category of "integration" is reduced to points of response to a Likert-type scale of instrumental choices. Thus, the interpretation and reflection are no more than mechanical and instrumental acts that are situated in the natural attitude. Husserl himself addresses the dilemma and its definition. Every *ego cogito* considered "something," a *cogitatum* (the thing that is apprehended by the ego. The *cogitatum* can be the Library's catalog, the call numbers used to locate physical items, the contents of a journal that help with finding a specific work. The *cogitatum*, though, can be the categorial nature of classification systems or the intentional meaning of the author of a work. These *cogitatio* are of different kinds. "He who attempts to doubt is attempting to doubt 'Being' of some form or other, or it may be Being expanded into such predicative forms as 'It is,' 'It is this or thus,' and the like... He who doubts, for instance, whether an object, whose Being he does not doubt, is constituted in such and such a way doubts *the way it is constituted*" [emphasis in original] (Husserl, 1962, § 31, p. 97) .

The phenomenological attitude represents what may be the most radical departure from the information literacy orthodoxy. It is different in kind from the course construction, standards, and pedagogy that is most frequently spoken and written about in librarianship. Also, it is difficult—first for the instructors, and then for the students. One aspect of the difficulty stems from the actuality that phenomenological cognitive action is, in many ways, remote from the natural way of perceiving and Being of each of us. We all exist within a strong tendency to live and perceive in an existence framed by our immanent surroundings, the world as it appears at the time of its appearance. Because of the immanence of the natural world, the world of our intentionalities tends to be likewise naturalized. In short, we tend not to doubt; *epochē* tends not to occur to us. For this reason *epochē* has to be cultivated as an attitude. To reiterate, many course and writings on instruction include "reflection," but reflection is situated only in the natural attitude. It does not contain the constructive doubt that enables the subject to contemplate the truth of something.

Here is an example that I hope will clarify the distinction between the natural and the phenomenological attitudes. A student is required to search for information relevant to a topic of her choosing, as part of an assignment in an instructional course. This is a typical kind of assignment that is meant to connect what happens in class to the Standards. At one level the assignment can be placed within the natural attitude; it can, for the student, be a test of the use of limiters, placement of terms in fields, and presentation of the output of the search. All of those things are needed for the student to comprehend the structure of a database of the mechanics of search algorithms. This is an exercise aimed at the student's learning about those instrumental features. The student's understanding of the protocols and how to manipulate them can be assessed and, if need be, further instruction, remediation, and correction can occur. Once the student becomes more proficient with the "natural" search and retrieval mechanics, something else can become the intentional focus of instruction. Before a term is entered, the student can begin to reflect upon the question that forms the application of the search. That is, the student can contemplate what is known and what is not known. The very nature of the question can be the locus of doubt. If the topic is something like, "What are the causes of violent crime in my home town," then each part—plus the whole—of the question can be subjected to transcendental reduction. Each part—causation, crime, violence, geographic location—can be reflected upon. In part, the need for the reflection is the creation of a complete understanding of what comprises each of the parts and of the whole. I am proposing here that the reflection is essential for both the search and the reading of the retrieved works to make sense. The essential character of the reflection is a necessary component of libraries' instructional programs.

This concentration on parts and wholes can be iterative as well. As the student examines—reduces—a published piece in an effort to apply doubt to the components, that student learns. One element of learning is the application of *epoché* itself; the experiencing of structured and purposeful doubt is something that must be learning through practice. Moreover, though, the student learns *from* the application of *epoché*. In subjected premises, propositions, and conclusions to doubt, the student can learn to revisit the initial question, and the search that is based on the question. The published work may help the student appreciate that the question is incomplete, for example. It may be that "cause" is not an appropriate concept to apply to the phenomena of violent crimes in a locale. "Cause" means something quite specific and limiting. "Contribution" or "contributory factors" may be more appropriate concepts to apply in the context of the rest of the question. If one seeks causes, and there can be no single discernible causes for the phenomena, the inquiry may be doomed from the outset. If there are discernible factors, then those should be the things sought. It may be that some specific violent crimes have contributory factors, while other crimes have different contributory factors. All of these things that can be learned can be applied to a revised question and, thus, to a revised search. From a practical point of view, students should learn that starting points in exploration are not final. In keeping with Husserl and the commentators on his thought, *epochē* is to be applied to *everything*.

Each retrieved work can then be subjected to *epochē*. Constructive doubt can be applied to everything an author of, say, a journal article contends. Every part of the article, every premise, proposition, and conclusion, that the author includes as comprising the whole of an argument can then be inspected and questioned. There is some technical language used in phenomenology to indicate the process at work. The student in this example, in questioning the parts and wholes of a specific article, engages in *noesis*, the act of becoming fully conscious of something. The thing perceived is referred to as *noema*. This is more than simply an object; it is the thing as (in this case) the author intended it. As such is embodies "how" the author used the particular object (premise, proposition, etc.). A *noetic* analysis entails the subject examining the acts of intentional construction, such as a proposed explanation of causes of violent crime (see Russell, 2006, pp. 84-89). Following Russell, Sokolowski, Zahavi, and Moran, I hasten to add that the process of *noetic* analysis is not an isolated ideal. It is an explicitly constructive examination of the intentional acts that are manifest *as part of* the objective world. In other words, I wish to affirm that we are dealing with the one world at all times, not separate *real* and *ideal* worlds. Examining intentionalities is, in phenomenology, the *only* way to reach a complete understanding of what is. This process, as described, is the genuine achievement of integrated understanding, of full appreciation of what others write, say, and show.

Learning of a more complete kind depends on cultivating the phenomenological attitude, as well as the natural one. As we can see, having the former is necessary to having the latter, but there is a separateness. Sokolowski (2000) is again invaluable here. In explaining the phenomenological attitude he makes the point that "The shift into the phenomenological attitude, however, is an 'all or nothing' kind of move that disengages completely from the natural attitude and focuses, in a reflective way, on everything in the natural attitude, including the underlying world belief" (p. 47). The reflection he speaks of is essential to *epochē*, the constructive doubt. By means of reflection and *epochē* we are able to contemplate ourselves in the world, ourselves with one another, and the world with ourselves in it. In other words, this aspect of phenomenology is the totality of the human physical worlds. As such it entails not just having the mechanics and materials that go into the building of a bridge, but also the human act of bridging—the reasons, purposes, fears, and desires that lead people to build a bridge from here to there. The "reduction" that is often mentioned in phenomenology is the action of constructive doubt; it is taken from the Latin for "withholding." The things we contemplate, that we have intentions regarding, are held in suspension pending *epochē*.

As a summing up of evaluation, I will emphasize that the key to learning of the kind I am speaking of here is reflection. The constructive doubt, the *epochē*, which is necessary to phenomenology, must be an explicit component of courses, including those that are part of libraries' instructional programs. While initiating this reflection in first-year college students is difficult, the process of initiation can begin in libraries' courses. In the next chapter, a suggested basis of content for a course, the opportunities for reflection will be inserted. The shift to a phenomenological attitude can begin for students as they examine what others write, say, and show. The shift can be incorporated into the kinds of things that may well occur in many courses. When students are asked to evaluate, for example, the claims in a journal article, the process of reflection can be documented, at least to some extent, by the students. In addition to composing an evaluation, students can record how they begin to question the author, how they make demands on those who make the claims. These responses, which can accompany a number of assignments that are likely to comprise the assessment in courses, can open a window onto the doubt to which the students are subjecting the works they read. The instrumental components of assignments (identifying elements of citations, locating specific works, etc.) can certainly remain so that the students' natural attitudes are also enhanced. The important thing to note here is that there is no set rubric for the assessment of students' application of *epochē*; as Sokolowski says, it is an all or nothing action. That said, it is indeed possible to recognize it in students' reflections. It may be necessary for instructors to engage in *epochē* first, then to introduce it in class.

Institutions and Phenomenology

The instructional program applications of phenomenology described above are extremely important to the entirety of this book. The applications do not end there, though. Everything that has been talked about here—constructive doubt, seeking knowledge and truth, reduction, subjectivity—apply to libraries and college and universities as well. The concept of Being can have institutional means, especially insofar as the institution fosters the phenomenological attitude as integral to mission and as essential to its own operation. Libraries, colleges, and universities themselves "speak;" they are responsible for utterances that must be examined in order to be understood. Because they issue utterances, they can be subjected to *epochē*. The vision statement of Grinnell (IA) College states: "We see the library as the campus gateway to an increasingly busy and evolving world of texts, images, and sounds. We see ourselves, our collections, and our facilities as a vital academic resource for every department, every staff member working together to meet the ever more complex needs of the campus community" (http://www.lib.grinnell.edu/general/mission-policies/libraryvision.html). If one were to examine every aspect of that statement there could be questioning en route to discerning the truth of the statement.

Paul Ricoeur (1976), who also was strongly influenced by Husserl, speaks to the kind of challenges that face us as we attempt to interpret what is said: "The concept of meaning allows two interpretations which reflect the main dialectic between even and meaning. To mean is both what the speaker means, i.e., what he intends to say, and what the sentence means, i.e., what the conjunction between the identification function and the predicative function yields. Meaning, in other words, is both noetic and noematic" (p. 12). Ricoeur (1976), in his brief work on interpretive theory, hits upon a very important element of *epochē*. Anyone who reduces (withholds judgment) on anything that is said, written, or shown has a task ahead of her or him. A work, for example—a journal article that a student is reading, a library's vision, a university's mission statement—embodies two loci for interpretation and, so, doubt. One is the statement itself, its apparent semantic structure, its diction, its syntax. This element is complicated by polysemy, the fact that a single word can have multiple meanings. Context usually lessens the challenge of polysemy, but it does not eliminate it. The second is authorial intentionality; the writer meant *something* in composing the statement as it has been conveyed. The second locus is the more challenging, since an author can dissimulate, can deliberately introduce possible meanings that are not intended.

The application of phenomenology to institutions is fraught with possibilities of deception.

So what does a library mean when it says it is committed to user education? In his introductory text Sokolowski (2000) uses the example of looking at a cube from one standpoint to illustrate the limitations of traditional interpretation. From that one place a person may see a square, or may see three trapezoids, or some other set of shapes. From only one place the person cannot fully comprehend the cube. However, moving perspectives, when combined, can provide a much more accurate perception. Ricoeur (1976) says, "The text as a whole and as a singular whole may be compared to an object, which may be viewed from several sides, but never from all sides at once. Therefore the reconstruction of the whole has a perspectival aspect similar to that of a perceived object" (p. 77). One way to resolve what may seem to be a dilemma here is to remember that the phenomenological attitude, when applied, makes all perspectives present to the perceiver. The natural attitude limits us to one standpoint at a time; the reduction of the phenomenological attitude transcends the natural limitations as we move about through multiple perspectives. The phenomenological attitude permits us to consider the institution as well as the learning that occurs within the institution.

I have a reason for introducing the institutional side of things here. The library, the college, or the university can create an orthodox presentation of what constitutes purpose and the means for achieving the purpose. A university, for example, can valorize a certain kind of empirical inquiry and can then define discovery according to the very limited definition of the one, method-based, stance. Legitimacy can then be attached to that location, with the corresponding action of attaching illegitimacy to other locations. When method achieves this kind of supremacy, the institution succumbs to a virulent kind of *unreason*. There is no reduction, no withholding of judgment, since judgment has been co-opted officially by the institution. *Epochē* becomes an endangered, if not extinct, species. One of the stated values of the University of Missouri is "Discovery," defined thusly: "Learning requires trust in the process of discovery. Discovery often fractures existing world views and requires acceptance of uncertainty and ambiguity. Therefore, the university must support all its members in this life-long process that is both challenging and rewarding. As we seek greater understanding and wisdom, we also recognize that knowledge itself has boundaries—what we know is not all that is" (http://www.missouri.edu/about/values.php). Acceptance of uncertainty tacitly denies *epochē* and, in doing so, denies an entire program that is aimed at uncovering truth.

The bottom line is that, for learning to be possible (and not only for students, but for *everyone* involved in the educational endeavor) there must be an institution that is just. The justice for which the institution stands is a mediating force; it instills the search for knowledge through an ethical framework. Paul Ricoeur (2000) writes, "Without institutional mediation, individuals are only the initial draft of human persons" (p. 10). His dictum applies especially to teachers. It is the teacher's responsibility to mediate; given that students are developing in all ways, the development cannot be left to accidental or opportunistic factors. The phenomenological attitude, as an example, is fundamentally *different from* the natural attitude (which itself requires guided development). The outcomes we desire from education do not simply occur, they are themselves intentional acts on our parts. If our colleges and universities are committed to knowledge and truth, then some overall institutional mediation is needed. By this I mean that, beyond a classroom or a course, the entirety of the college or university should embrace the phenomenological attitude when it comes to itself. The constructive doubt of *epochē* is needed for continued commitment, and commitment through action, to knowledge and truth. To use Husserl's language (and not in the altered form created by Heidegger), the institution must create the lifeworld that makes phenomenology possible. If the college or university falls short in any way in achieving the institutional goal, the library, and librarians, must step up.

Summary
The preceding forms a preface to the culmination of the critique begun in Chapter One. The project will be completed in the next chapter. There I will articulate possible content—and reasons for the content—that can comprise a course. It would be arrogant even to hint that the suggested content is the only way to achieve programmatic goals; the content presented should be taken for what it is, one conception for a course in a libraries' instructional program. It may be that the particulars of the content are far less important than the spirit that I hope is transmitted through the structure of a course. It is that phenomenological spirit that is intended.

CHAPTER SIX

Putting it All Together

The detailed description of phenomenology in the last chapter sets the stage for some consideration of the actual content that might comprise a library's course. The goal for the course (and this is a goal that could only minimally be realized in one or two class sessions) is to imbue students with the sense of phenomenological cognitive action. In particular, the goal is to augment students' natural attitudes with the phenomenological attitude. As is evident from the foregoing discussion of first-year college students, the phenomenological attitude will not become a part of students' Being by means of a one-credit course. The course, though, along with purpose-driven general education require-ment, can help achieve the goal. In the course students, with the help of the instructors, can begin to explore what *constitutes* knowledge, and how knowledge differs from belief. The course—in presenting what information is, how it is located (in multiple sense of the word), and how it is comprised of separate but related things—introduces students to an action that Sokolowski (2000) emphasizes: "The *attempt* to doubt, however, *is* subject to our free choice. We can attempt to doubt anything, even the most obvious fact before us or the most established opinion [emphasis in original]" (p. 55).

I do want to stress that the necessity of phenomenological cognitive action does *not* mean that the understanding of information structures and the ability to navigate structures are not vitally important (just as the natural attitude is vital to the phenomenological attitude). The course content that will be presented here demonstrates, I hope, the interweaving of the information structures and the apprehension of the contents. In fact, an aim is to place the students in the midst of the structures and the contents. Comprehension of how the contents of information packages (especially scholarly contents) are created, produced, and disseminated is one means of situating the students. The ultimate aim is to create in students the ability to *obtain* information (informing works) for the purpose of creative learning. The course is a step along a pathway (the entirety of a student's academic program). The ultimate aim includes assisting with students' development—intellectually, cognitively, philosophically, and ethically. That is, the aim is to enable every person to grow in Being and to be able to pursue knowledge and truth. As Sokolowski (2000) says, "'Being' is not just 'thing-like': being involves disclosure or truth, and phenomenology looks at being primarily under its rubric of being truthful. It looks at 'human' being as the place in the world where truth occurs" (p. 65). This aim is ambitious; the aim of libraries' instructional programs is to take that first step on the pathway.

The following is a suggestion for the content of a credit-bearing course (likely to comprise one credit hour). It is, of course, no more than a suggestion, which means that components or specific elements detailed here can be rejected as not relevant for a particular setting. Some items could be replaced by others; some could be adopted as is; some could be greatly revised. The aim of the suggested content is to embody phenomenological cognitive action by presenting students with an integrated means of learning from what others write, say, and show. The learning is enhanced by the students putting the thoughts of others to work in their own assignments, courses, and programs. The purpose of the suggested course content is the development of a sound experience for students whereby they become better equipped to build their knowledge bases and to engage in critical assessment of the claims of others. Also, what is presented below can be adopted for single, or multiple, sessions in other academic courses. Specific needs or opportunities that the courses represent might be addressed by aspects of the course outline and content. For example, a class session could emphasize the categorial nature classification systems as a means to assist student in their search for texts that can help answer the questions they frame. Specific examples of ways the course content can be applied in instructional sessions in disciplinary courses are noted below, and are set off textually by brackets.

Beginning the Course
The first step in the course is to communicate the operational goals

that are to be achieved by the end of the semester/session. The goals themselves can be stated in a fairly straightforward manner:

1. Enhance students' ability to frame meaningful questions.
2. Gain knowledge and skill to succeed academically.
3. Understand the structure and content of information resources.
4. Become able to evaluate the information that is out there.
5. Use information resources as genuine learning tools.

The course goals, of course, are necessary to students' understanding of the course, but they probably are not sufficient. Students will need to know where this course fits into the entirety of their academic programs. One tactic that can be considered is beginning with a question: Who wants to earn good grades, not only in the class, but in all of them? That can be followed up immediately with the question: How are you going to earn good grades? Some connections to practical benefits are most likely to capture students' attention. Emphasize strongly that the course will help them save time and effort and to do their work more efficiently and effectively. This course will reduce students' costs while increasing their benefits. They will accomplish this by:

- being able to break down [reduce] the components of assignments and questions
- understand which of those components they need to know more about
- select the most appropriate place/source to find out more about that component
- search for the bits of information they most need
- evaluate the information they retrieve
- use that information to complete assignments and answer questions

Note: Instructors can tell students that the purpose of this course is to present ideas, strengthened by providing hands-on experience, which will be useful throughout their college years. "Information" may be something that they are aware of at some level, but they tend not to think about it much at this point in college life. If it has not already happened, their teachers will ask them to "find out about," or "locate an answer to," or "get resources on," some topic related to the class. The instructor may ask the class if their teachers have already done this. Beyond fulfilling the requirements of assignments, these sources from other people can enable everyone to become aware of things they were not aware of, to affirm data, and to think about some topics in ways they had not before. In order to find answers to questions they may be instructed to seek answers to, students should understand that reading or viewing the products of these other people's minds is something like a conversation, a dialogue. An author is speaking to someone; a particular author may be speaking to a particular set of people. An author of an article in a magazine like *Time* or *Newsweek* may be speaking to as many people as possible. In order to facilitate discussion it may be helpful to distribute copies of an article that has recently appeared in popular magazine.

Also by way of example, an author of an article in something like *Baseball Weekly* is speaking to a smaller and more focused group of people. It may be helpful to bring copies of an article to class. As everyone in the class reads the article each student may question the author: What made you come up with this idea? Why did you ask the question this way? How are you coming up with the conclusions you reach? Why did you use the particular evidence you did, and not some other sources of evidence? Are you genuinely seeking an answer, or are you trying to convince me of something in particular? What may be the most pertinent question for the students is: What is the author saying to *me*? In other words, one should take everything one reads or view at face value. This is a way to bring in, subtly, the phenomenological attitude. It is a point that needs to be made in this first class meeting; it is best to take the phenomenological attitude towards what authors present. This attitude should be emphasized now and throughout the course.

To bring the point of questioning home in the first meeting, the instructor can ask the students to imagine that they are about to buy a new car. Ask in particular, What specific things do you want in that new car? How would each of them go about finding out which care would have exactly what they want? The discussion can raise matters that would require becoming informed about the task of purchasing a car. Those matters can be tracked (by recording them individually, for instance) and taken up by the class. Another possibility is to say to the students: I will give you $75 to buy a new pair of shoes; how would you spend the money? How do they decide what kind of shoes to buy? A similar process of tracking and review can follow students' responses. The purpose behind the questions is to link questioning to mundane topics and tasks. This can heighten students' awareness that they are engaged in some sorts of questioning almost every day that they do engage in the natural attitude. Moreover, they may already be taking systematic approaches to finding answers that are meaningful to them.

Next Class Session

For the second class meeting a possibility may be to invite a faculty member who teaches undergraduate courses to attend class. The faculty member can state what he or she expects in class and what it takes to succeed. That person can emphasize the value of the library's course to meeting the expectations in her/his class. The instructor of the library's course can then talk about what these faculty members said and what was emphasized. The instructor can stress again that this course will help do what the faculty member talked about—doing things efficiently and effectively—and reinforce that effective learning leads to academic success when what is learned is applied diligently in courses. The final point that can be made in this part of the class meeting is that students will succeed when they seize the opportunity to learn, and do not simply fulfill the mechanics of assignments.

The next segment of the class meeting can entail looking at how we all think about questions. A major component of this class is the presentation of the importance of being able to frame a question. This seems simple, but clarity (on the parts of both the speaker and the listener) is vital and sometimes elusive. The instructor can ask students: What interests you? Why does it interest you? What makes you curious about something? One way to get the students to participate is to ask them to write down the answer to: What is one thing that you really care about? It may be that the students can then exchange what they write down with one another and then one student will use what is written to introduce the other student. This engages the students early on and gets them interested in each other and thinking about interests in general. The main point of this is to get students to understand that, if they really care about something, they go to considerable effort to find out about it. This could be taken this one step further: Ask the students where they go to find more about what interests them. Use what they care about to introduce something that they need to understand: Teachers will compel them to be interested in some things; to earn good grades and to save time, they need to be efficient in finding information about these things.

This class meeting may be a good time to get across to students that success, and also learning, requires action. They cannot wait passively for knowledge (which requires action) and expect to earn good grades. This course will help them take the action that will lead to effectiveness. At the end of this session the students can be given the assignment to respond briefly to the following two questions. Their answers can then be an opportunity both for understanding of the students and a source for discussion. In the next class meeting the responses can be reviewed. Also, these questions can be asked again in the last class meeting to see if the outlooks and responses have changed:

- **What is information?**
- **What is a library?**

The Landscape of Information

The third class meeting can feature the broad, deep, and complicated landscape of information—including how much is out there and where it comes from. It can begin with discussion of the questions from the last session's assignment. The instructor can then briefly demonstrate how much stuff is out there in some specific ways: Build on the first class session's tour; remind the students how much physical stuff is in the library, and that very little of it is available electronically. Get to the library databases page; demonstrate how many databases there are, and how much each covers. Illustrate the number of databases the library has access to; show how many hits a very simple library catalog search yields (e.g., History – United States); demonstrate how many hits a seemingly focused Google search yields (e.g., professional baseball).

This is a good opportunity to do a brief introduction to the catalog:

- To begin with, explain how to navigate the home page (how to get to databases, how to get to the catalog, etc.).
- Once in the catalog, explain the various fields and what they mean. This will mean a short treatment of Library of Congress Subject Headings (LCHS), for example.
- The instructor can talk a little about the advantages and disadvantages of keyword searching.

This introduction can be short, but should include an example of a search in each field, maybe especially points out the tips that are on each page. One can casually mention how many volumes are in the college or university library collection.

This session can be an opportunity to discuss where the amount of information comes from. This discussion then moves into the human element of information. The stuff that is out there is created by people, for people; that cannot be emphasized strongly or frequently enough. Newspapers, popular broadcasting, magazines, etc. illustrate creation of information to entertain and/or to provide news. Serious inquiry into topics is somewhat different, but is also a human and a social creation. Examples of faculty on campus can be used to show where ideas come from, what they do with the ideas, and how they communicate them:

Examples from the University of Missouri
Schulz, David J. (Biological Sciences)
Schulz, D.J., Goaillard, J.M., Marder, E. "Variable Channel Expression in Identified Single and Electrically Coupled Neurons in Different Animals." *Nature Neuroscience* 9 (March 2006): 356-62.

Roxanne W. McDaniel (School of Nursing)
Conn, V.S., Porter, R.T., McDaniel, R.W., Rantz, M.J., Maas, M.L. "Building Research Productivity in an Academic Setting." *Nursing Outlook* 53 (September-October 2005): 224-31.

Charles N. Davis (Journalism)
Davis, Charles N. "Expanding Privacy Rationales under the Federal Freedom of Information Act." *Social Science Computer Review* 23 (Winter 2005): 453-62.

John Miles Foley (Classics)
Foley, John Miles. *How to Read an Oral Poem*. Urbana: University of Illinois Press, 2002. PN1341.F65 2002

The differences in audiences (popular, scholarly, etc.) for published work can also be demonstrated. The faculty are communicating in particular ways, through particular outlets (e.g., journals), to particular people. This moment could be a good time to introduce the creation for audiences/conversations. The varieties of magazines and journals can be illustrated:

General	General/Topical	General/Special
Time	*ESPN the Magazine*	*Scientific American*
Newsweek	*Glamour*	*Psychology Today*
Wired	*Jazz Improv Magazine*	*Political Science Quarterly*

Academic/General	Academic/Topical	Academic/Special
American Scholar	*Science*	*Physical Review*
Daedalus	*American Literature*	*Financial Statistics*

It may useful to show where each title is indexed and point out the connection between the content of these sources and the places one goes to search for that kind of information.

This class meeting can also be an opportunity to introduce the differences in authorship (e.g., the author of a book that the library owns, authorship of a magazine article, authorship of a scientific article (multiple authors), or "authorship" of a Web site). The traditional concept of "author" can be discussed, as can co-authorship (two or more individuals sharing responsibility for work). That is, students can comprehend that an author takes responsibility for the content of the work. That person is claiming some authority, knowledge, and voice to express what she or he does. Authorship, in this traditional sense, is personal; an individual expresses something meaningful simply by *being* an author. At this point the idea of, say, sampling in music can be covered within this idea of authorship as an example of changing conceptions. Authorship in the academic sense frequently means staking a claim for an idea, a theory, or a solution to a problem. Researchers and scholars care very much that they receive credit for the work they do.

At this time the instructor can emphasize that the creation of information anticipates a question: For example, compilation of data on average rainfall assumes that people will want to know rainfall amounts for specific places; a long exposition on a political topics assumes that people will want to know more than data and will probably want to engage with the author (affirm, dispute, question, etc.). When people write or create things they tend to do so not just for themselves, but to communicate to others. Sometimes the communication is intended for "everyone," but many times the communication is intended for certain groups or niches. When students begin to take advanced courses in their majors they will have to become competent with some body of information. The present course puts them on the road to succeeding at becoming competent, or even proficient. Course titles in various departments can be used as examples of the kinds of conversations and audiences that exist at the university:

> **[At the University of Missouri]**
> Electronic Commerce Security
> History of the Family in Russia
> Heat and Mass Transfer in Biological Systems
> Latent Variable Models in Statistical Analysis
> Social Revolution in Latin America

The instructor can ask students to think about course topics of study in terms of what they plan to do after college (i.e., what do they think they will need to know for their anticipated careers; what do they need to ask about now in order to know that career-related stuff). The purpose here is to bring home that information use will always be able to contribute to their success, whether in a profession, or just becoming more knowledgeable about their interests.

[The content of this class meeting can provide a foundation for some of the kinds of single sessions that librarians present in faculty members' classes. The range of journal types can be used to illustrate the kinds of treatments in disciplines. A more popular science journal, for example, can be introduced in class, as well as a more special-ized or advanced title to show students the different audiences for the work. The session can also introduce students to the concept of "author." In more advanced work in various disciplines the assertion of a new idea or the staking of an intellectual claims are extremely important—academically and practically. In some fields staking a claim might enhance the possibilities for attracting external funding for future research.]

Information Content
The fourth class meeting can begin with a couple of items that might be mentioned in the news (newspapers or magazines); the instructor could bring a newspaper or magazine to class. Copies can be made for the students and they can be asked:

- Were you aware of this (the topic of the item) in general?
- Are you familiar with the particulars of this piece?
- What questions does it raise for you?
- How would you transform that question into a search?
- Where would you go to find out answers to your question?

At this point there can be an in-class exercise with actual execution of the searches. The exercise can entail revisiting the array of available databases; demonstrate that there are subject guides that can help searchers identify databases in particular disciplines. The databases searched can be documented, as can the search strategy used. Some of the results of the search can also be discussed by the class, in terms of the above questions.

When encountering things that are within a students' general awareness (even though the student has not seen the facts before) there is an essential act of evaluation that should occur. That is, the new information should be assessed on several grounds, and the grounds should be rational. This warning applies to the wording of assignments that instructors give to students. Here is something for instructors to consider: John Searle writes in *Rationality in Action* (2001): "Consider any situation of rational decision making and acting and you will see that you have a sense of alternative possibilities open to you and that your acting and deliberating make sense only on the presupposition of those alternative possibilities" (p. 15). Searle's quotation is introduced here as a reminder to everyone that the education process in general is necessarily a rational action. When considering, for example, ways of completing assignments, students have choices among various ways of responding. The rationality of this particular situation constrains possibilities in several ways. Instructors in various courses provide not only general, but also specific, instructions. Instructors may give clues as to what must be included, what must not be included, indications of time (the most recent information available as opposed to histori-cal data), indications of specificity (an entire population of an area, or subsets of the population—such as only males, only left-handed people, only lawyers, etc.), or other specifics. These instructions provide ways of creating search strategies that incorporate the specifics (ANDs, ORs, and NOTs). Academic Search Premier can be used for the examples. Suppose an assignment were given in another class to find informa-tion on health care to infants in Africa. A search: "health care" AND infant* AND Africa (all default fields) results in 76 hits (28 March 2008). The number on 1 June 2006 was 53. If "Full Text" and "Scholarly (Peer-Reviewed) Journals" is added at the beginning, the number is 38 (it was 28 on 1 June 2006.

Evaluation has to presuppose that a piece of information will be deemed convincing in any number of ways, or not. Choosing the evaluate it one way or another requires that there be multiple possible ways of interpreting it. In other words, accepting one piece of information (or an idea, claim, etc.) simply "because" is not rational. Phenomenology, and most of epistemology, insists on consistency and coherence. Something that is written and published should be internally consistent; it should not have contradictions. It should also make sense syntactically and grammatically. In short, students can question what they read. They can look closely at things are stated. For example, they can examine the difference between saying, "Poverty is the cause of violence in urban areas," and "Poverty is a cause of violence in urban areas."

- What is the difference between the two statements?
- Suppose you were assigned the task of finding support for the first statement; what would you do?
- Same for the second statement.
- Do searches in class to try to discover more about each statement.

The discussion that follows can focus on the difference between the two within the context of framing a question, and then formulating a search to answer that question.

Here is a possibility for homework for the next class. Students can go into a grocery store. They are to: Examine the arrangement of the store. Locate peanut butter. What do you find (kinds, brands, sizes, etc.)? What is near the peanut butter? How are those nearby products related to peanut butter? Locate grape jelly. How close is it to peanut butter? How many brands of grape jelly are there? How many sizes of grape jelly are there? What other jelly flavors are there? What else is near the jelly? Now, what do you see with regard to the arrangement—would you be interested in nearby products if you're looking for peanut butter or jelly; are there some identifiable categories of nearby products; can you locate peanut butter and jelly easily? They should take notes for discussion in the next class. This is an exercise that is intended to enhance the natural attitude. "Peanut butter" and "jelly" are known to the students, but they may not have thought explicitly about variations, combinations, and choices.

[Again, there is the potential to draw from this general class meeting to devise customized presentations in single or limited sessions in courses. The stating of possible questions in a variety of ways can be translated into searches in disciplinary databases. The statements above related to poverty can be altered to be pertinent in any number of courses. The bullet points can be used in the class session. The students can come to understand that the meaning of search results will be connected to the meaning of the questions asked. In particular, the students can develop a sophisticated appreciation for the ways that logical connectors can be employed to specify the kinds of output that may be retrieved.]

Categorization

In the fifth class meeting the concept of categorization can be introduced; we classify and categorize things all the time—easy vs. hard courses, good vs. not-so-good beer, attractive vs. less attractive people. These categories affect what we do and how we do it. The key to finding things (anything) is to figure the order by which they are organized. In general, things can be categorized in any number of ways—by size, by color, by shape, by function, etc. When we categorize things for ourselves we tend to do so according to our own uses of the things. In a kitchen we may put the most often used spices in the handiest place. This is organization for use. We may also categorize things so that we put like things together. Linnean taxonomy is an example; see http://www.paleos.com/Systematics/Linnean/Linnean.htm. This is a hierarchical categorization, but this is not the only way to organize things. Categorization can get quite complicated, in large part because the things we want to categorize can be complicated. If something is big, blue, round, rough-textured, heavy, and mobile it could be categorized by any of the features.

The homework assignment from the previous class meeting (peanut butter and jelly) can be discussed at this time. Students will have gone into a grocery store and paid attention to the arrangement of the store. What brands, types, and sizes of peanut butter and jelly are there? What is next to them and why? Why might things be separated? What sorts of store guides help you find something? For example, students can be asked what they do when they enter an unfamiliar retail store. Do they look for signs; do they have ideas in mind of what to look for? The differences of these schemes can be examined; an exercise in class could involve categorizing one set of things in various ways (this may even be books by size, color, paperback versus hardback, topic, etc.). The next step is to explore how we express these differences among and within categories. What words are used to describe categorization by function as opposed to by form?

After the discussion, the class can move on to categorization of ideas. The instructor can now introduce categorizations by "aboutness," or content. Categories describe physical things, but how do they describe ideas? An exercise can be to distribute a brief article from a magazine such as *Time* or *Newsweek*. The class can discuss how they would tell others what the article is about. One way to do this is to give the article to every other person and have the reader tell the other person, using only single words or short terms, what the article is about. The goal is to arrive at practical and useful categories (that is, categories that could be used as structured terms). The subject headings used in the library catalog entry for the book can then be shown to the class, and students can discuss the merits and/or shortcomings of those subject headings. They might suggest how they would describe the book. *This is an opportunity to return to the library's catalog and focus for the time being on subject searching.*

Example:
Brown, John Seeley and Duguid, Paul. *The Social Life of Information.*
Information Society
Information Technology—Social Aspects
How useful are the subjects for finding books like *The Social Life of Information*?

Next, the instructor can introduce the ways things are already described. Show examples of subject headings for books, thesauri, "browse" functions in databases, etc. Introduce the concept of a controlled vocabulary. LCSH or a thesaurus can be passed around to give students an idea of how people and organizations have built vocabularies to describe things. The difference between a controlled vocabulary and keyword searching can also be introduced. Two different databases may use different descriptors for the same item.

> **Example:**
> [from Academic Search Premier]
> Calabrese, Andrew. "The Promise of a Civil Society: A Global Movement for Communication Rights." *Continuum: Journal of Media & Cultural Studies* 18 (September 2004): 317-29.
> **Subjects:**   Civil society
>   Communication
>   Communication policy
>   Consensus (Social sciences)
>   Social contract
>   Sociology
>
> [from Sociological Abstracts]
> Same article
> **Subjects:**   Civil society
>   Rights
>   Communication policy
>   Participation
>   Social Movements

[Note: This article is used only for illustration of differences in subjects/descriptors.]

It is clear that a couple of the terms are the same, but there are several differences. Each database does its own indexing, so there is no universal standard. This creates some challenges, so we all have to be aware of the differences from one database to another, even with the same items. With the examples, instructors can explain to students that tools already exist to describe information. People have tried to describe what books, articles, etc. might be about and created resources to help with the description of the "aboutness" of those things. Make clear to students that most of these resources have been created independently from one another, so the words used to describe ideas can vary from one resource to another. It may even be that variation is inevitable, since each reader may focus attention on different particular aspects of a work. Sokolowski (2000) observes, "In categorial activity we articulate the way things are presented to us; we bring to light relationships that exist in things in the world" (p. 95). He further states, "It is no longer a simple state of affairs for me; it is now, for me, a state of affairs *as being presented by you*; this qualifier makes it into just your judgment, not the simple fact" [emphasis in original] (p. 99).

Along with the subject headings, instructors can demonstrate the differences in classification (call numbers). There is no need to go into much detail; one can emphasize the major point that call numbers are not merely addresses. If it is possible to have the students go into stacks and browse during the class, this may bring the nature of classification home to them.

Example: PS signifies American literature
PS991-3390 signifies nineteenth century
PS2124 signifies Henry James

The following are some possible exercises that could be employed either in class or as homework.

- A practical idea of categorization needs to be introduced in a way that students can grasp quickly. The Linnean taxonomy site can be used as a demonstration in class. To bring the point home, bring some object into class. It could be a ball, a shoe, or a tool. Get the class talking about the ways the object can be categorization—shape, color, size, etc. Also ask about functional categorization, such as the purpose of the tool, the sport in which the ball is used, what the shoe might be good for. Ask the class if the function helps, not only describe, but categorize the object.
- Subject searching in the catalog can be introduced here. The above Brown and Duguid book can be the example. Illustrate the record for the book and explain the subject headings. These are intended to categorize what the book is about. The subject headings can be searched and the students can be asked if these works might be like the Brown and Duguid book. The specific language of LC Subject Headings can also be explained. The Calabrese article can also be used as an example of categorization. Demonstrate the record in

Academic Search Premier; search the assigned subjects to
see if there are articles like the Calabrese one. Then move to
Sociological Abstracts and show those subjects and search
for related articles. Illustrate the first ten or so hits in each
database to see if there is any duplication. The point students
need to get is how working from the same starting point in
different databases can yield different, but useful, results.

[Categorization, of course, applies across all fields. Examples of categorization can be incorporated into segments of instructional sessions.
An article from a more specialized journal in a particular discipline
could be introduced in the class and students could proceed through
the interpretive processes outlined above. Possibilities for interpretation
in specialized areas may be more limited in one sense (the universe of
content in one field is not absolutely extensive), but there may be much
more subtle gradations in categorical interpretations. Application of
the interpretation could be used to point students towards the need for
careful subject searching in specialized databases.]

Packages of Information

The next proposed topic, packages of information, may well occupy
two class meetings. There is a lot to cover here, including the ways information can be packaged by form or by content (and the differences
within each) and the reality that where one looks for information will
affect what one will find. The instructor can show students the various
possibilities among information containers. "Package" can be taken
literally here, even in a virtual environment. Form, in this case, can be
defined as the amount of information available in a package. A book
may contain a great deal about one narrow topic, or it may address
many topics (for instance, a book may contain a collection of essays by
a number of authors). It may be great in depth or great in scope. Parts of
a book may be suitable for some purpose and may help you learn more
about something specific. For example, the instructor could bring in a
book and show students the index. The index and the notes or references
can be shown to be analogous to hyperlinks. Demonstrate navigating
from index and notes to the text of the book. On the other hand, an
article will usually address a small topic in some depth. An article can
also include a bibliography or references. The book demonstrations can
be repeated with an article.

Each student, in every instance of fulfilling an assignment, must decide how much he or she will need/want to know about a topic. In the first couple of years in college the need may be for a limited amount of information on a specifically targeted topic. The instructor can ask the students if they have a textbook of one of their other classes with them. Have them look at it and see how it refers to other works. The textbook author may have to draw from prior work. An assignment in some class may define the need; it may specify precisely what is to be addressed. One may become curious about the topic and may want to know more. When looking for background information there are a number of choices. Teachers may help put the assignment in a particular context or time or place (or perhaps they should; as Head and Eisenberg (2009) observe, they may not always provide context). Once each student begins serious work in a major area of study, the need for information may deepen. The types of packages are simultaneously ways of categorizing content; the following examples can illustrate the categorization:

Examples: Handbook used for reference
Textbook (introductory)
Collection of essays
Book on a single topic
Special issue of a journal (all on one topic)
Journal article
Web site with lots of links to other sites
Web site devoted to one topic

The students can examine what are the differences among the packages when it comes to communication—how much is communicated, how it is communicated, to whom it is communicated. For example, one question students can address is how much one needs to know in order to understand fully what's in the package. The last point raises another packaging issue. A more popular magazine (*Psychology Today*, perhaps) assumes that the typical reader is not a specialist in psychology. The magazine is packaged to appeal to a broader readership. It would be a good chance to reinforce the ideas of audience and conversations here to illustrate what kinds of packages are generally geared to which audiences or which kinds of conversations.

To illustrate the point, the instructor can bring in a copy of something like *Psychology Today* or *Scientific American*. Read the beginning of an article and ask if the students can follow it. Then read from an article in a specialized scholarly journal. Can they follow that? Which one is more likely to be "speaking" to them? The scholarly journal is aimed at one audience having a particular kind of conversation. The popular magazine is aimed at a different audience having a different kind of conversation.

At this time too it would be appropriate to delve a bit deeper into databases. The point can be made that these databases are gateways to information that is packaged in particular ways. For the most part they allow access to the journal literature, but not exclusively. Academic Search Premier might be a good source to use consistently, but not exclusively in the course. Maybe the first thing to point out is that the records are treated "equally;" there is no obvious distinction at a glance what type of package a specific item is included in. For the purpose here the various formats of materials included in the database can be demonstrated.

The task in class could be in the form of teaching the students how to "read" the database. It is possible to interrogate or question a database. The instructor can ask where the article appears (what is the title; is it a popular publication; is it a technical journal). One can ask some things about the author (who is this person; what is her/his position; what institution is the author affiliated with; what else has the author written).

Example: The entry from Academic Search Premier for the Calabrese article (above) can be used to demonstrate the subjects again, the abstract and how to read it, and the author's affiliation (his "authority").

This is a good opportunity to delve into the structure of Academic Search Premier. It is possible to conduct a basic or an advanced search. It is possible to limit the results by type of publication, date, or full-text. If their assignment in another class is to include three scholarly articles, you can show them how to search specifically for scholarly articles. The following can be done in real time in class:

For example, the students can search for items on "communication policy."

First: they can enter this as a basic search.

Second: they can enter it in advanced search mode (no difference).

Third: they can enter it as a subject (far fewer).

Fourth: they can narrow by date (say, January 2001 to date).

Fifth: they can limit to scholarly journals (becoming more manageable).

Sixth: they can limit to full text.

The students can be asked what the differences are. The progressive reduction in hits can become readily apparent.

Exercises: For the first exercise use a database that fits well with the majors of some of the students in the class—psychology, history, biology, etc. Get students to suggest a topic to search; demonstrate the search in the appropriate database. Ask students to choose an article from the retrieved items and then use available tools that can enable them to find the article. When an article is retrieved, go through what it communicates: title, authors, authors' affiliations, source (journal), and references. Ask the students what each of those elements says to them. Is the author from a reputable institution? What does the person cite? Another opportunity is to work through the "communication policy" example above in Academic Search Premier. Involve the students at every stage.

In continuing coverage of the packages of information, one tactic is to get students to talk about something that could have more than one audience. When authors write, they frequently have an audience in mind—a group of people that they're trying to communicate with. This is evident in the discussion in the last class session. There is another way that authors communicate to audiences; they refer to previous works that their readers may be familiar with. In other words, they use background, or cited, works to establish a context for their own writing. This audience-based communication establishes something of a network of thinkers who share some common ground. The works of others also point to another key characteristic of phenomenology: "Our ability to shift propositional reflection allows us to take a distance toward any issue we are involved in" (Sokolowski, 2000, p. 188). Reading the other works can involve the act of reflecting on their ideas in conjunction with one's own.

This may also be an appropriate time to introduce the idea of the network. The books, articles, Web sites, etc. that are accessible are not to be taken as isolated, independent pieces; they all relate and interrelate. The searching homework from last time can be referred to as a way that individual works can be networked together by common subjects. This is a loose network, but there are tighter ones. Books and articles may both help to answer questions and to point to other sources that may answer questions. The packages of information, while individual, form a kind of network. The pieces of the network build on one another, refer back and forth to each other, and confirm or deny what each other says.

Example: This maybe the place to emphasize the usefulness of the citation. As was mentioned in an earlier class session, an analogy may be to look at the citation as a hyperlink. In some databases this is literal; one can click on some references and move to the full text of the cited article. Another analogy is the reference list of an article or book as database; it is a targeted secondary source that can lead to additional useful information. As an example, search Business Source Premier. Search "advertising" in Subject and "automobiles" in Default Fields. Click on Full-text and Scholarly (Peer-Reviewed) Journals. Then in the retrieved documents, one can click on "cited references" for one of the articles. Demonstrate that students can get to those articles. If they are reading the citing article they can find a cited article that appears to be relevant.

One way to expand the idea of network, have students search for some teachers' names in Academic Search Premier (and be prepared to suggest some names of faculty members from one's own institution to search Explore the database feature that points to times cited. If some faculty have written multiple works, ask students to examine these titles. Do they form some cohesive whole? Do topics vary? Where do the faculty publish? Are there indications of writing for different audiences or for different conversational purposes? One purpose of this exercise is to point out that author's names can be searched, as well as subjects. If they find that one person has written a very useful work, they can see if that person has written any other works that might be useful.

Exercise: Demonstrate the cited references tool in the EBSCO family. Use the example above in Business Source Premier. With prefacing remarks on how and why people cite (drawing from assignments students may have had that include using secondary sources), explain how the tool works (with the students following along in the database). What results is a set of practical and intellectual connections; the citing works form a kind of network with the cited work. There must be some kind of connection between them. The tool can help prompt a question in students' minds: What do other people think about what this author has to say? There can then be additional questions that arise. To what extent do others agree or disagree with the cited author? What are the bases of their disagreements? What can I learn from the diversity of views?

[Instruction regarding the meaning and uses of citations can be a component of instructional sessions at all academic levels and in all fields.]

Making Sense of the Web

Perhaps one of the most pressing challenges in any instructional program is helping students understand what, in fact, the Web is, what it contains, and how best to make use of it. One element of the challenge is the accurate gauging of how much detail to provide. A smattering of history will probably help illustrate the genesis and evolution of internet-based resources.

A practical next step is coverage of commonly used search engines. Google, or any search engine, may be seen as a packager of information. Every time one searches Google, it harvests bits and pieces of what is out there and packages it. It may be an excellent tool for finding data on something, such as the scores of ball games, statistics on players, populations of places, process of goods, etc. It may also be good for informing one of when and where things happen. This may be as immediately useful as show times for a movie, or dates of events in the past. That basic feature can and should be demonstrated in class, using topics that students themselves suggest. The purpose of the demonstration is not so much to enlighten students (they probably do search for times and locations of things), but to illustrate how kinds of questions kind be categorized.

To bring this feature home to the students, an in-class exercise could be introduced early on in the first session on the Web. This exercise may involve identifying the kinds of "when,"" where," and" how many" questions such as movie times or news, and then ask students to go to their favorite sources for the information and search for answers. Something that is in the news at the time of the class meeting might work. Ask where they would go for that. When they get there, ask them to identify the source of the information. Then go to a second source and compare the reports. A variation could be to do a Google search on a current event. The students can then exam the first few hits: Who is reporting? What is the person's affiliation? Who sponsors the site? Is there agreement on the content among the various sites? The class can discuss the findings, thus adding an evaluative element to the exercise. If there is disagreement about interpretations, or even facts, aspects such as authority can be explored, multiple sites can be viewed so as to identify agreement, and the natures and kinds of disagreement can be defined. Sokolowski's example of viewing a cube (mentioned in the last chapter) could be introduced in this class to illustrate both the possible limitations of perspective and the need to transcend those limitations.

Search engines, in general, operate in very similar ways. Harvester bots mine Web sites for occurrences of words, for example. One way some engines make money is by selling ads; frequently the ads are connected to your search (you search for advice on the care of puppies and the site for PetSmart pops up). Sometimes, as with Google, the pay sites are (at the time of this writing) identified first in a manner that ostensibly distinguishes these advertising sites from the body of retrieved hits. The class can be asked about these sites at the time of introduction; a purpose is to assess the extent to which students comprehend the placement of such advertising sites. Another method of harvesting is based on what other people have linked to their own sites. The more times others have linked to a site, the more likely that site may show up when you search. You might ask, though, if what you want to see is what other people have seen. Searching exercises can help students see these factors. Students could search for information on topics that are pertinent to other courses they are taking and then gauge the importance of the retrieved sites to those topics.

As an exercise to understand differences, everyone can conduct a particular search a few different ways: A topic such as music downloads can be conducted in Google, and a couple of other engines. The results can be compared to those of an advanced search in these engines ("music download" AND (economics OR copyright)) would be a possibility. To illustrate further difference, the directory structure of a resource like Yahoo can be used with this same topic. Also, Google Scholar can be searched and, again, the results can be compared. The key point to make here is that the "Web" is a generic thing; there are ways to get much more specific. Also, the comparison among the different search engines can illustrate that each one packages information somewhat differently. This can generate some discussion in class.

With these search exercises it will be important to spend some time on the results, the hits resulting from the searches. Students can be asked to rate the top five (or so) hits according to the degree to which each really does address music downloads. They might also determine the ways these sites are addressing music downloads—legal issues, how-to advice, suggestions for selecting download services, etc. Then the advanced search results can be rated according to how completely each item addresses more specific topics, such as the economics and/or copyright of downloading. The same can be done with other search engines and possibly with Google Scholar. In the course of reviewing the results, the students should discuss the audience for each of the items and the conversation that each item appears to be immersed in. That is, they can determine the purposes to which the specific sites, and the information the sites convey, can be put; making decisions about downloading music necessitates a process that is different from selecting sites to be used in a course assignment.

The source of each of the evaluated items should be identified at a simple level. That is, students should determine (for example) if a particular site is a commercial one selling download software or offers an interface for the downloading of music, or if the site is examining some particular aspect of music downloading. Is there a hierarchical ordering to these different sources in the results list, especially moving from general to advanced searches, to other search engines and Google Scholar? One particular outcome would be for the students to discuss which hit they believe, and why. That is, what criteria would they have for placing credence in any particular hit? The University of California at Berkeley has developed a site entitled, Teaching Library Internet Workshops: http://lib.berkeley.edu/TeachingLib/Guides/Internet/FindInfo. html The Berkeley site, especially the "Evaluating Web Pages" section, can be demonstrated in class, or it can be homework. Students can be required to view the workshop and respond to a few questions that are imbedded in the site. For example, one assignment question can be, "What are the three key questions to ask related to part 2 of the site?" And also, "What factors should be considered in answering 'Why was the page put on the Web' (part 5)?"

Exercise: Bring in a news item from the last month or so (try to bring in something that was big news). Use the news item to show how some questions can be generated from a brief account of something (background on people, places, events, etc.). Have students search for information on the news item in Google. The first order of business is to ask how they searched (the terms used, connections, limits, etc.). Then ask about the first page of hits—do they appear to be pertinent to the topic; what is their source; what is the authority of the site? Ask if the sites agree on the aspects of the item (such as the above background). Discuss the results. Incorporate the "Evaluating Web Sites" portion of the Berkeley tutorial into the examination of the Google results. As was the case with a citation, ask students to examine the pieces of a site to see what each communicates to them. That communication is essential; evaluation is more than an examination of the content itself, but includes the other information that indicates reliability, among other things.

It is almost certain that one fifty-minute class meeting will not be adequate to cover even the most fundamental matters concerning the use of Web-based resources for academic purposes. The primary purpose of a second class session is to urge students to evaluate the Web—and search engines such as Google that harvest from the Web—as only one of many resources they can use to learn more and to succeed in all courses. Comparisons can be made between Web resources and the kinds of things that databases include.

Now that the students have experienced searching databases, it is time to examine some differences between them and Web search engines. The idea of "container" should be reinforced here. A database, even a large aggregator like EBSCO, selects on some basis what will be included. In this way it is a relatively small, and more easily labeled, container (that is, we can name what Sociological Abstracts, for example, is about). To illustrate further with Sociological Abstracts, get into the database and click on the question mark (?) that follows "Now selected." There's a description of it. How large a container is the Web? Can we label, or name, it? This packaging is, for the most part, by subject area for databases. The packaging is indiscriminate for the Web as a whole. Another thing to emphasize is that, with all types of containers, things can come and go (journal titles can be added to and dropped from a database; sites disappear from the Web, at least at some levels).

This is where the construction of the Web's content can be introduced. Students can be shown how easy it is for something to be added to the Web, to the container (it is expandable). The growth rate can be used to demonstrate how rapidly the container is expanded. Refinements, like Google Scholar, that have been demonstrated in the previous class meeting can now be delved into as a different kind of container. It no longer is everything; it is a subset. For example, today (21 February 2009) I searched Google, advanced, "music download copyright," all the words; there were 49,400,000 hits. The same search structure in Google Scholar results in 81,000 hits (one year ago there were 35,300 hits). The basic question that can be asked of students here is: Why search the Web and why not a database? How does the nature of the question influence which container you'll look in?

To reiterate and expand, Google has a particular algorithm to determine in what order the retrieved hits are displayed—PageRank. Google own site states:

> PageRank relies on the uniquely democratic nature of the web by using its vast link structure as an indicator of an individual page's value. In essence, Google interprets a link from page A to page B as a vote, by page A, for page B. But, Google looks at more than the sheer volume of votes, or links a page receives; it also analyzes the page that casts the vote. Votes cast by pages that are themselves "important" weigh more heavily and help to make other pages "important."

Important, high-quality sites receive a higher PageRank, which Google remembers each time it conducts a search. Of course, important pages mean nothing to you if they do not match your query. So, Google combines PageRank with sophisticated text-matching techniques to find pages that are both important and relevant to your search. Google goes far beyond the number of times a term appears on a page and examines all aspects of the page's content (and the content of the pages linking to it) to determine if it is a good match for your query.

It might be useful to get into a particular database and list the titles that the database covers, including the dates of inclusion. This listing can illustrate two thing: (1) how many titles a big database includes (how much stuff it contains), and (2) the years of coverage of the titles, demonstrating the titles are added and dropped over time. If one has access to ArticleFirst, then the Browse Journals and Newspapers feature can be demonstrated; one can demonstrate from the alphabetical list how extensive the coverage is. JStor could also be used as a demonstration. One can click on About JStor, then follow the trail to the complete list of journals.

Exercise: This session presents an opportunity to reinforce the purpose of academic success. The Web is enormous; it is true that there is useful information that is part of it, but it is also true that there is unreliable, even false, data. Demonstrate that Google has several tools that comprise the whole. Google Scholar is one tool that is intended to help students and faculty. Spend part of the class getting students to search Google Scholar. If assignments in other courses can be worked in here, please do so. The students can use what they have learned so far to evaluate what they get from their searches. Points including source, authority, etc. apply here. Have them look at the retrieved items to see if they come from journals that might be included in other databases. In particular, ask students if Google Scholar is as effective a tool for their needs as the databases that the library provides access to.

[The essential points related to the variability of the content available via the Web can be a component of many instructional sessions. Evaluations of Web searches compared with database searches can bring home the need to retrieve reliable information. Something to emphasize is that content retrieved on the Web is by no means necessarily useless or unreliable; there can be connections to work that scholars and researchers are engaged in. If the session is aimed at some of the physical sciences, the site, http://arxiv.org/, could be introduced as a location of preprints of scientific papers. The notion of authority applies to almost all discussions of the Web.]

Relevance

Translating "relevance" into something real people can understand is a chore. In our profession we tend to think in terms of relevance, but that thinking may not translate to this group of students. Students, however, do want to find meaningful information that is connected to what they want to know/do. Finding something meaningful requires thinking about what might be some criteria of information. This is only a starting point, but it is an essential one; a search cannot be designed without some criteria. Starting with topical relevance—something retrieved is relevant if it is related to the topic of the search. Imagine a continuum of relevance, from "not" to "extremely." Everything retrieved falls somewhere along the line.

Example: Someone has a question about the ways that the US Supreme Court makes decisions. Searching "law" is too broad (search in a database). Progressively narrow the search—"courts," "supreme court," "United States Supreme Court," etc.

The example illustrates how much may be retrieved depending on the breadth or narrowness of the search entered. Here is a chance to reinforce the importance of framing a question. The starting point of any query is not possible search terms, but what the searchers wants to find out. This means it is very important for the students to give some thought before searching to the nature of an assignment, the requirements for a paper, etc. Most importantly, this is a chance to demonstrate to the students that if they spend some time and effort conceiving what they want/need to know at the outset, they can save time and effort further down the road. As an example of using tools to help frame the *search* once the question is framed, the subject tool in Academic Search Premier can be shown. Entering "law" provides pointers to more specific, or related, terms.

A challenge is how to place something along a relevance continuum. An in-class exercise can allow students to make assessments based on titles of works, on the subject headings/descriptors assigned to the works, and to abstracts of the works. They can be asked which is more helpful, which best provides clues to topical relevance. Return to the music download search; have the class examine the first ten hits. A purpose here is to demonstrate that determining relevance is not an easy matter. Discussion can focus initially on words in the title, then students can compare those to the descriptors. The abstract can come next; look for different words that might help with decision making. Students can compare words that appear in the abstract with the descriptors. To extend this exploration, the next step can be to look at the reference list. What words appear in the titles of cited works? What does the author say about these cited works ("Here is some additional stuff," or "This work is groundbreaking"). This also re-enforces the idea of network; not only is the "what" of citation potentially helpful, so is the "how." An analogy here may be movie reviews. The citing author is, in a sense "reviewing" previous work.

Another key point to make is that it is extremely rare (sometimes impossible) to find an item that is "perfectly" relevant; that is, there is not likely to be an article, book, etc. that has all of the topical elements of a search. However, there may be many items that have *some* of the topical elements.

Example: A search in Academic Search Premier of Twain AND Stowe AND race (all in the default fields) yields no hits. A search of Twain OR Stowe AND race yields more than 2,600. Many of those items are potentially relevant; they just may not be *completely* relevant. Again, looking for relevant content in this broader way can save time and also can help produce a better paper that will earn a better grade. This search can be done by the students in the class so that they can see what kinds of things are retrieved.

It is no simple matter to figure out if something is meaningful. Finding something meaningful can be based initially on the criteria, but it is also important to be open to what is retrieved. An item retrieved may suggest something that the student had not thought of, and may prompt an alteration in thinking. Suppose the searcher does not know much about the topic; how does that person make the decision? Is it possible that potentially useful items may be passed over because they do not immediately register as topically relevant? Most undergraduate students may feel a bit inadequate; they may believe (and may be led to believe by high school and even university teachers) that they *should* have this knowledge beforehand. It is important to enforce that the lack of knowledge is much more common. What this means in practical terms is that every item retrieved in a database search and every site retrieved in a Web search carries questions, as well as answers. Further, in practical terms it usually means that one item (one journal article or one Web site) is likely to be insufficient; there is not enough context to evaluate it fully. Sokolowski (2000) asserts that some principles to guide evaluation: "There is something pragmatic about propositional reflection. We execute it in order to find out more accurately what is the case. If we find out that the proposition is true, we accept it again, with the new, stronger evidence that the confirmation brings, but if we find out it is false, we reject it" (p. 190).

At this point the instructor can introduce a fairly complicated topic that is in the news but that people may not know a lot about. Couch it in terms of an assignment: Write a short (3-page) paper on reasons for the slowing of the U.S. economy at the same time the inflation rate is rising in 2007. Now ask the students to approach you as a though you were a reference librarian. How do they frame questions that would help them complete the assignment successfully? Emphasize that librarians are extremely valuable resources who work to help them succeed.

One thing that students need to understand is meaning can be created, as well as found. This segment of the course builds upon what has been said earlier about a particular kind of weak constructivism. That is, each of us must understand, integrate, evaluate, and consolidate what others write, say, and show. The process does not entail creating meaning out of whole cloth, but assimilating the complicated body of information that exists and that is retrieved. We make connections between and among bits of information and ideas that enable us to see two or more seemingly unrelated things in new ways. Each citation, each abstract, each document is interpreted the first time we see them. But they are also reinterpreted as we read more citations, abstracts, and documents. For instance, when we read a second document there may be questions raised about the first document. We may then re-read the first document and interpret it differently. This is the *noetic* process that is central to phenomenology; in part, when works are read the process entails uncovering concealment or deceit. That concealment or deceit exists lends credence to the need to develop a phenomenological attitude.

Example: The first document retrieved on the topic of the budget of the United States says, "The deficit for the present year's budget is not important; as a percentage of the total budget this deficit is lower than the deficit of 1987." That can be interpreted and seen as meaningful on its own. Then the second item retrieved states, "While the deficits in some past years have been smaller as a percentage of the total budgets, this year's deficit (in real dollars) is higher than it has ever been and the interest that accumulates on the deficit is also higher than it has ever been—both in real terms and as a percentage of the total budget." How does the second statement lead to a reinterpretation of the first one?

How do we figure out the criteria for meaningful information? One criterion related to this topic is authority. If information is going to be trusted, you may want to know on what basis someone speaks. Has the author done work in this area before? Does the author appear

to know how to investigate the topic? Authority may also have institutional connection. For example, an item retrieved may be a report
by a panel of experts. It is still important to examine the institutional
source. Is this a political institution? Is it a partisan group? Source also
affects authority. Is a blog as authoritative as a peer-reviewed journal?
In short, might concealment or deceit by employed by a source? An
exercise in peer reviewing may be appropriate. It may be easier to
find information that agrees with your viewpoint on the Internet,
since this is an open environment. That said, remember that some
Web content is paid for by someone. Also, bloggers may not always
be true to data and evidence. An exercise here may be to point to two
bloggers on the same topic but taking different stances. The question
can be asked, "What do you look for in an article or a book that helps
you decide that it's meaningful to your project?" The instructor can
write the ideas on the board and then ask how the students put these
into practice.

One element may be something like, "the author is a professor at
Harvard," or "the author is a member of the President's Board of Economic Advisors." The next step can focus on the person (author). The
author may have also written X books and Y articles on this subject.
(Both the affiliation and the past record speak to the author's authority.)
Especially in the sciences a journal article may note that the work was
funded by a federal agency, a foundation, or a corporation. Students
can be asked if there is a difference related to authority with these
three sources of funding. The journal of the publisher may also speak
to authority. The journal's editor and editorial board can be examined
(this can be the first step in explaining peer review).

Example: The Web is an enormous container with a very wide
mouth and no obstructions. A subject such as intelligent design might
be used here. A Web site for the Institute for Creation Research (www.
icr.org) might be used for illustration. One of the Institute's scientists
is Russell Humphreys, who argues that the earth can be no more than
100,000 years old. Humphreys' argument can be analyzed, along with
other works that refute those arguments. To expand discussion into the
political realm, it could be mentioned that President Bush said publicly
that intelligent design should be taught along with evolution.

Peer Review is a particular structure that is intended to help with
evaluation of content. A thorough explanation of peer review can be

found at the Wikipedia site: http://en.wikipedia.org/wiki/Peer_review. While it may seem ironic to some that a Wikipedia entry can be used for this purpose, the site could be viewed in class. This can be the topic of the homework assignment. Question 1—What are some reasons why peer review is used? Question 2—What are the four customary recommendations that referees make to editors?

[The exercises described above can provide some indicators of discussions that could be introduced in disciplinary instruction sessions. That is, the types of searches and evaluations can be adjusted for students studying a variety of subjects at any level. The introduction of peer review may well be appropriate to the courses in which the sessions occur.]

Looking for the Who and the Where
Habits of practice can begin with this course and be carried on throughout each student's academic career. For example, when students begin serious work in their majors they should be aware of what else an author has said. This requires finding other works by the author in question. Consistency of thought, while not necessarily a virtue, may be important in a discipline. It might also be important to see growth in thought, deeper assessment of issues, more mature thinking about topics, etc. Also when students are taking courses in their majors, they should be aware of what others say about an author's work. This is a step in critical skepticism. When assessing what others write say, and show there are some key elements to keep in mind.

The questions that Myron Tuman (2002) urges be asked can be integrated into this class meeting. Each of the questions can be asked as part of an in-class discussion of issues that are in the news or that may occur in the assignments for other courses. For example, his first questions, "1. Who is speaking to us? Who is the author of this information?" can be applied to the specific items that are retrieved. Students can identify the piece's author(s) and the affiliation(s). An article may also include a bit of biographical data about the author(s) [a faculty member from one's institution might be used as an example]. His next question is, "2. What biases does this author exhibit, and what sources is the author using?" This entails reading the article for the point of view of the author(s). For instance, the beginning of the article might assert some assumptions from which the author(s) proceeds. The students can discuss whether the discussions are warranted or whether the assumptions themselves should be inquired into. Next Tuman asks, "3. Why is this author promoting this position?" Discussion can inquire into any policy or action recommendations that author(s) may have or into any statements that suggest an ideological stance. The fourth question is, "4. Where does this information appear, and what interest does this entity have in widely disseminating these materials?" The class can examine the source; the publisher or producing organization can be identified. Lastly, "5. How recent is the article itself as well as the sources it uses?" The question contains the guidelines for examination.

The first three numbered questions may make immediate sense; if someone is writing from a particular point of view; that may be a clue to the author's purpose. Number 4 may not make intuitive sense; the class can discuss why Tuman includes this? The same applies number 5; does it matter if the sources cited are new or old?

At this point, there can also be an in-class assignment on a controversial topic where there can be two clear and divergent ways of approaching the topic.

Example: Two brief pieces on evolution and intelligent design are introduced. What is at the heart of each argument?

> Betty, Stafford. "Intelligent Design Theory Belongs in the Classroom. *National Catholic Reporter* 42 (October 21, 2005): 23.
> Shipman, Pat. "Being Stalked by Intelligent Design." *American Scientist* 93 (November/December, 2005): 500-02.

Another exercise may be to demonstrate searching for commentary about a specific author in a field of study (maybe a local faculty member). Agreement and disagreement may well become apparent. Related to this exercise is figuring out what the nature of disagreement is, and why people disagree. This can mark a return to evidence and its interpretation. It can also serve as an introduction to normative interpretation. This is not to say that an orthodoxy should prevail, but that there should be legitimate grounding for a particular interpretation. So much for the author, what about the things other people say about what the author has written? In just about any field of study an author's intentions in publishing something are multiple. One purpose is to claim to be correct about something. Another purpose is to engage in a conversation. Others in that field have a formal record of what the person said, so they can use that work in their own, affirm it through their own research, or refute on any of several grounds.

The citing author may make explicit reference in a publication: "Jones made the erroneous claim that X is true. My work demonstrates that Y is true." "Truth" can be somewhat elusive. There may be some things to look for, though, that can help decide on accuracy and reliability.

- Authority
- Design of the study
- Logic employed in the work
- Recency of the research
- Mathematics or statistics
- Cited works

In the case of disagreement, one may have to decide whom to believe. Before you decide on which author may be correct, you have to be constructively skeptical; that is, you should not be ready to side with one person because of connections, reputation, etc. While authority is a very useful learning and evaluation tool, it is not absolutely reliable. Experts can be wrong; just because they were right in the past does not make them right this time. This also hearkens back to an earlier session where we discussed that there is going to be some uncertainty given that each of us has some lack of knowledge. Experts can also have a lack of knowledge, and they may have a purpose not really related to knowledge. They may be trying to persuade readers to believe what they have to say because of political, religious, or other reasons.

Sound evidence is useful both for the establishment of validity in arguments and for finding the truth of propositions. The evidence for validity is the internal logic of all of the propositions (premises and conclusion(s)). The evidence for the truth of propositions is much more complicated, and information is an essential tool in uncovering that truth.

Example: Let us say that if developed countries send financial aid to countries in Africa, those countries will be able to work themselves out of poverty. The premise can be examined on the basis of evidence. One can look at data available in information resources to investigate the effects of financial aid to African countries in the past, especially the recent past. If the data do not demonstrate that aid assists countries in reducing poverty, the premise may be questionable. Students can search Academic Search Premier: "foreign aid" AND Africa AND poverty. They can the look at the first page of hits to see what evidence is offered in the works for the conclusions that are reached.

[The content of this class meeting lends itself directly to the more limited time librarians have with students in instructional sessions. This content may also represent an opportunity for the librarians to work with the faculty to design a session that builds upon students' existing knowledge. The students can be urged to exercise critical judgment regarding the work in their major fields; the faculty member might suggest conflicting ideas and then the librarian can introduce ways to search for and retrieve materials that can be used to assess the ideas.]

Ethics and All This Information

Plagiarism is probably the most common ethical problem in higher education. An effective assumption at the outset is that students at this age are not fully aware of what plagiarism is. Now that they have some experience finding information and evaluating it, the time is ripe to demonstrate proper appropriation of the information into their own work. There are examples of famous people who have been caught plagiarism—Stephen Ambrose, Doris Kearns Goodwin, and others—these should be shown in class. The most important thing to communicate to students is that, if the work of someone else shapes their thinking, they should acknowledge that person's work. The most obvious use is of quotations from other works. Acknowledgement does not end there, though. It extends to ideas. If something you read suggests a different way of thinking about an issue, you should acknowledge it formally. Beyond plagiarism, there is the requirement that work that is represented as being your own must in fact be your own. An exercise here would be to work through a policy on student behavior. The University of Missouri's policy on academic dishonesty is: www.umsystem.edu/ums/departments/gc/rules/programs/200/010.shtml

Acadia University's (Nova Scotia) interactive tutorial on plagiarism can be introduced in class: http://library.acadiau.ca/tutorials/plagiarism/. The tutorial can be a component of the class session and then a discussion of the points can follow. It can generate some specific questions about the right and wrong ways to incorporate others' work into our own.

It can now be the appropriate time to revisit the questions that the course began with:

- **What is information?**
- **What is a library?**

Students will once again turn in their answers. The differences between the responses at the beginning and at the end of the course can illustrate what students have learned and how their attitudes may have developed.

[Every instructional session provides an opportunity to introduce, or reinforce, the importance of ethical behavior. The need for proper attribution and recognition of others' ideas and words can be emphasized, frequently by articulating the home institution's guidelines regarding academic honesty.]

Course Wrap-up

It is not just by seeking and finding information that we learn; reading and seeing can be a learning experience. When you take what you do know, and seek to add new information that can lead to new knowledge, success is enhanced. The textbooks that are used in courses may be the most straightforward example of learning by reading. Likewise, the process of writing creates a learning event. Through writing thoughts down they can become somewhat separate from themselves. They can then be re-read in a new light. The habits of practice are meant to last throughout one's college career. Before long students will be taking courses in their major. The expectations for performance and the measures of success will become more stringent. Regardless of the subject matter, evaluation will still be essential. An exercise could be getting students to think of a basic topic in their anticipated majors. They could think through (and search for) evidence for multiple perspectives on the topic. They could then weigh the alternatives, see on what is the evidence based, and outline the next steps. Constructive doubt will be reinforced here. The key is to look deeper until the skeptical attitude cannot be sustained. Throughout the course there has been a background emphasis on reading, and on paying attention in general.

Writing also is a means of discovery. Students can be told that putting thoughts onto paper or screen involves a critical process. In completing the assignments of this semester students have had to communicate thoughts through writing. Sometimes that has meant that they have incorporated the thoughts, ideas, and arguments of others. Students can reflect on how they have thought about these other ideas and on what that has done to their own thinking. These steps they have taken may help prepare them to think, write, and work in their majors. The instructor can then return to the discussion of the planned or anticipated majors. Students should reflect on how this course relates to doing work in those fields: What will constitute propositions in that field; what does a valid argument entail; what evidence supports both propositions and arguments? Now, what information sources will help you locate the evidence you need to make the above judgments?

This is a time for questions, particularly about the writing process as a means of discovery. Have the students think about writing as a way to think through an assignment, a topic, a way communicate what they know, and a way to integrate the information they find through the search process. Ask them especially how they learn from what they write. This exercise is intended to emphasize and reinforce reflection.

Perhaps most important in this last session, the students can be asked what they have learned that will help them succeed throughout their academic programs? What things that were covered have had an immediate impact? What do they think has helped them with assignments in other courses? What is still unclear? Is there anything they wish they had been exposed to?

Summary

As is stated above, this course is a suggestion. Also, the course content includes suggestions for instruction in settings other than a full, semester-long course. It has been developed, though, within the context of phenomenological cognitive action. The formal presentation of the course content in such detail here may be useful in the building of a course to be offered as part of any library's instructional program. Perhaps, more importantly, it can enhance conversation on instruction in general and can contribute to further developments of librarians' contributions to learning on their campuses.

Epilogue

I have attempted to argue in this book for a different conception, and a different application, of instruction programs in academic libraries. Some of the received views of information literacy have difficulties that may not be overcome by minor alterations to standards or orthodox statements. The critique that has been presented here is intended, not as an attack on work that has been done, but as a revision that builds upon prior thinking and practice. In other words, what is presented here owes a debt to predecessors, and some of the predecessors that have contributed most directly to the ideas in this book are acknowledged. That said, a premise that has guided the ideas here is that some substantive changes should be made. The changes include the language and discourse that are used in our professional literature. Discursive practices in any profession should be open and should assess what is said on the merits of what is said; such a guideline must apply to instruction.

A particular framework is developed in this work—phenomenological cognitive action. The framework is, admittedly, a complex one, but it holds potential for the development of programs and instructional sessions that are aimed at enhancing the understanding of students. The framework explicitly recognizes the cognitive challenges that students face, challenges that threaten overload and confusion. What is frequently referred to as critical thinking requires complex logical, intersubjective, and emotive processes. The actions of articulating questions, searching, retrieving information, and evaluating what is written, said, and shown are far from simple, so students must learn to appreciate the complexity, and the demands the actions make on them. Articulating a question necessitates a level of understanding that enables the questioner to posit relationships among factors, recognize similarities and differences, and anticipate outcomes. From that standpoint searches can be formulated and texts can be assessed according to the questions asked. The possible modes of instruction are integral to phenomenological cognitive action, so the particular pedagogical methods and theories of teaching employed must be fitted to the forms of cognitive growth that are intended by instructional programs. The suggestions in this book are by no means the final word, but they are meant to be taken seriously as groundings for instruction.

While certainly not the final word, the foundations of this book include the goals of student learning. The goals include integration of all institutional plans and experiences that are intended to help students learn and grow. Libraries' instructional programs and sessions are not isolated activities existing for any ideological or self-serving purposes. They are components of a holistic learning environment. The phenomenological element of the suggested framework is particularly intended to contribute to the holism. Understanding is an outcome of actions that have been detailed by Edmund Husserl and other philosophers. One of the actions is that of metacognition—thinking about thinking. The self-critical thought that students can be taught to engage in is an invaluable aid to the more complete apprehension of what others write, say, and show. Emphasis here should be on the reality that students can indeed be taught, at a rudimentary level, to apply metacognition as they proceed through articulating questions and the other necessary steps that constitute the intentional use of information. As is shown in this book, the teaching can occur, to a considerable degree, by means of examples. The examples can be unique to an instructional program, but (and this may be more effective) can be drawn from other courses that students are taking.

All of the background leads to the suggested prototype course. The course is based on a set of objectives that relate to the growth and learning of students throughout their academic programs. The progression of the course is intended to begin with the most fundamental intellectual acts and proceed through more complicated and interconnected ideas. Of necessity, the course includes the structures and workings of resources, including print and electronic information packages. The effective use of the resources is a prerequisite to retrieving useful texts. There is more to the course, though; the workings of class meetings and exercises draw out from students a collective and individual comprehension of the ways of thinking of the words and images that others have offered. In short, a goal is to assist students along the road to thinking informationally. The outline of the prototype includes suggestions that could be incorporated into single class sessions in the courses offered by other departments. The goals remain the same, whether the presentation of a single class or a semester-long course.

Ultimately, the intention here is that the present work will contribute to the development of instruction in academic libraries. Libraries' instructional programs are currently making substantial contributions to student learning on hundreds of campuses. The potential for growth in learning, though, is enormous. Perhaps this book can lead to conversations that lead to the realization of the potential.

References

Albitz, Rebecca. 2007. "The What and Who of Information Literacy and Critical Thinking in Higher Education." *portal: Libraries and the Academy* 7, no. 1: 97-109.

Andrade, Heidi Goodrich. 2000. "Using Rubrics to Promote Thinking and Learning." *Educational Leadership* 57, no. 5: 13-18.

Association of College and Research Libraries. 2006. "Information Literacy Competency Standards for Higher Education." http://www.ala.org/ala/acrl/acrlstandards/standards.pdf.

Association of College and Research Libraries. 1989. "Presidential Committee on Information Literacy: Final Report." http://www.ala.org/ala/acrl/acrlpubs/whitepapers/presidential.cfm.

Bakhtin, M. M. 1993. *Toward a Philosophy of the Act.* Trans. by Vadim Liapunov. Austin: University of Texas Press.

Bakhtin, M. M. 1986. *Speech Genres and other Late Essays.* Trans. by Vern W. McGee. Austin: University of Texas Press.

Bloom, Benjamin S. 1984. *Taxonomy of Educational Objectives. Boston:* Allyn and Bacon.

Bok, Derek. 2006. *Our Underachieving Colleges* (Princeton: Princeton University Press.

Bok, Derek. 2003. *Universities in the Marketplace: The Commercialization of Higher Education.* Princeton, NJ: Princeton University Press.

Booth, Wayne. 2004. *The Rhetoric of Rhetoric: The Quest for Effective Communication.* Malden, MA: Blackwell.

Bourdieu, Pierre. 1991. *Language and Symbolic Power.* Trans. by Gino Raymond and Matthew Adamson. Cambridge, MA: Harvard University Press.

Bourdieu, Pierre, and Passeron, Jean-Claude. 1994. *Academic Discourse: Linguistic Misunderstanding and Professional Power.* Trans. by Richard Teese. Stanford: Stanford University Press.

Bransford, John, Sherwood, Robert, Vye, Nancy, and Reiser, John. 1986. "Teaching Thinking and Problem Solving: Research Foundations." *American Psychologist* 41, no. 10: 1078-89.

Buckland, Michael. 1991. *Information and Information Systems*. Westport, CT: Greenwood.

Budd, John M. 2009. *Higher Education's Purpose*. Lanham, MD: University Press of America.

Budd, John M. 2007. "Information, Analysis, and Ideology: A Case Study of Science and the Public Interest." *Journal of the American Society for Information Science and Technology*, 58 (December): 2366-71.

Burke, Gerald, Germain, Carol Anne, and Xu, Lijuan. 2005 "Information Literacy: Bringing a Renaissance to Reference." *portal: Libraries and the Academy* 5, no. 3: 353-70.

Buschman, John. 2009. "Information Literacy, 'New' Literacies, and Literacy." *Library Quarterly* 79, no. 1: 95-118.

Churchland, Paul M. 1995. *The Engine of Reason, the Seat of the Soul: A Philosophical Journey into the Brain*. Cambridge, MA: MIT Press.

Churchland, Paul M. 1988. *Matter and Consciousness*, rev. ed. Cambridge, MA: MIT Press.

Clydesdale, Tim. 2007. *The First Year Out: Understanding American Teens after High School*. Chicago: University of Chicago Press.

D'Angelo, Beverly, and Maid, Barry. 2004. "Moving Beyond Definitions: Implementing Information Literacy across the Curriculum." *Journal of Academic Librarianship* 30, no. 3: 212-17.

Davidson, Donald. 2001. *Essays on Actions and Events*. Oxford: Clarendon Press.

Davidson, Jeanne and Crateau, Carol Ann. 2000. "Intersections: Teaching Research Through a Rhetorical Lens." *Research Strategies* 16

Dennett, Daniel C. 1991. *Consciousness Explained*. Boston: Little Brown.

Dennett, Daniel C. 2005. *Sweet Dreams: Philosophical Obstacles to a Science of Consciousness*. Cambridge, MA: MIT Press.

Descartes, René. 1989. *Discourse on Method and the Meditations*. Trans. by John Veitch. Buffalo, N Y: Prometheus Books.

Doherty, John J and Ketchner, Kevin. 2005. "Empowering the Intentional Learner: A Critical Theory for Information Literacy Instruction." *Library Philosophy and Practice* 8: no. 1: http://www.webpages.uidaho.edu/~mbolin/.

Dretske, Fred I. 1981. *Knowledge and the Flow of Information*. Cambridge, MA: MIT Press.

Eco, Umberto. 1984. *Semiotics and the Philosophy of Language*. Bloomington: Indiana University Press.

Educational Testing Service. 2005. "Beyond Technical Competence: Literacy in Information and Communication Technology." http://www.ala.org/ala/acrl/acrlpubs/whitepapers/presidential.cfm.

Educational Testing Service. 2002. "Digital Transformation: A Framework for ICT Literacy. A Report of the International ICT Literacy Panel." www.ets.org/Media/Tests/Information_and_Communication_Technology_Literacy/ictreport.pdf.

Egan, Margaret and Shera, Jesse H. 1952.

Elmborg, James K. 2006. "Critical Information Literacy: Implications for Instructional Practice." *Journal of Academic Librarianship*. 32, no. 2: 192-199.

Elmborg, James K. and Sheril Hook. 2005. *Centers for Learning: Libraries and Writing Centers in Collaboration*. Chicago: ACRL.

Emmons, Mark and Martin, Wanda. 2002. "Engaging Conversation: Evaluating the Contribution of Library Instruction to the Quality of Student Research." *College and Research Libraries* 63, no. 6: 545-60.

Farber, Even Ira. 2007. *College Libraries and the Teaching/Learning Process: Selections from the Writings of Even Ira Farber*. Richmond, IN: Earlham College Press.

Fodor, Jerry. 1998. *In Critical Condition: Polemical Essays on Cognitive Science and the Philosophy of Mind*. Cambridge, MA: MIT Press.

Fogelin, Robert. 2003. *Walking the Tightrope of Reason: The Precarious Life of the Rational Animal*. Oxford: Oxford University Press.

Foster, Andrea L. 2007. "Information Navigation 101." *Chronicle of Higher Education* 53, no. 27: A38-A40.

Foucault, Michel. 1972. *The Archaeology of Knowledge and the Discourse on Language*. Trans. by A. M. Sheridan Smith. New York: Pantheon Books.

Foucault, Michel. 1998. "What Is an Author?" In *Aesthetics, Method, and Epistemology: Essential Works of Foucault 1954-1984, Volume 2*, pp. 205-22. Trans. by Josué V. Harari and Robert Hurley. New York: New Press.

Freire, Paulo. 1970. *Pedagogy of the Oppressed*, trans. by Myra Bergman Ramos. New York: Herder and Herder.

Gallagher, Shaun. 2005. "Phenomenological Contributions to a Theory of Social Cognition." *Husserl Studies* 21: 95-110.

Gazzaniga, Michael. 2005. *The Ethical Brain*. New York: Dana Press.

Gibson, Craig, ed. 2006. *Student Engagement and Information Literacy*. Chicago: ALA.

Glasersfeld, Ernst von. 1995. *Radical Constructivism: A Way of Knowing and Learning*. London: Falmer Press.

Goffman, Erving. 1974. *Frame Analysis*. New York: Harper.

Goldman, Alvin I. 2002. *Pathways to Knowledge: Public and Private* (Oxford: Oxford University Press.)

Goldman, Alvin I. 1999. *Knowledge in a Social World*. New York: Oxford University Press.

Goodman, Nelson. 1978. *Ways of Worldmaking*. Indianapolis: Hackett.

Grassian, Esther S. and Kaplowitz, Joan R. 2001. *Information Literacy Instruction: Theory and Practice*. New York: Neal-Schuman.

Green, Donald P. and Shapiro, Ian. 1994. *Pathologies of Rational Choice Theory: A Critique of Applications in Political Science*. New Haven: Yale University Press.

Gross, Melissa. 1998. "The Imposed Query," *Reference & User Services Quarterly* 37, no. 3: 290-99.

Gross, Melissa. 2005. "The Impact of Low-Level Skills on Information-Seeking Behavior: Implications of Competency Theory for Research and Practice." *Reference and User Services Quarterly* 45, no. 2: 155-62.

Gulllikson. 2006. "Faculty Perceptions of ACRL's Information Literacy Competency Standards for Higher Education." *Journal of Academic Librarianship* 32, no 6: 583-92.

Habermas, Jürgen. 1998. *On the Pragmatics of Communication*. Ed. by Maeve Cooke. Cambridge, MA: MIT Press.

Habermas, Jürgen. 2001. *On the Pragmatics of Social Interaction: Preliminary Studies in the Theory of Communicative Action*. Trans. by Barbara Fultner. Cambridge, MA: MIT Press.

Head, Alison J., and Eisenberg, Michael B. 2009. "Finding Context: What Today's College Students Say about Conducting Research in the Digital Age." Seattle: The Information School, http://www.projectinfolit.org/pdfs/PIL_ProgressReport_2_2009.pdf.

Hempel, Carl G. 2001. *Philosophy of Carl G. Hempel: Studies in Science, Explanation, and Rationality*, ed. by James H. Fetzer. New York: Oxford University Press.

Hirsch, E. D., Jr. 1988. *Cultural Literacy: What Every American Needs to Know*, updated edition. New York: Vintage Books.

Hofer, Barbara K. 2004. "Epistemological Understanding as a Metacognitive Process: Thinking Aloud During Online Searching." *Educational Psychologist* 39, no. 1: 43-55.

Horgan, John. 1999. *The Undiscovered Mind: How the Human Brain Defies Replication, Medication and Explanation*. New York: Free Press.

Hrycaj, Paul. 2006. "An Analysis of Online Syllabi for Credit-Bearing Library Skills Courses." *College and Research Libraries* 67, no. 6: 525-35.

Husserl, Edmund. 1999. *Cartesian Meditations: An Introduction to Phenomenology*. Trans. by Dorian Cairns. Dordrecht: Kluwer.

Husserl, Edmund. 1970. *The Crisis of European Sciences and Transcendental Phenomenology*. Trans. by David Carr. Evanston, IL: Northwestern University Press.

Husserl, Edmund. 1962. *Ideas: General Introduction to Pure Phenomenology*. Trans. by W. R. Boyce Gibson. New York: Collier Books.

Iser, Wolfgang. 1978. *The Act of Reading: A Theory of Aesthetic Response*. Baltimore: Johns Hopkins University Press.

Jackson, Norman. 2004. "Developing the Concept of Metalearning." *Innovations in Education and Teaching International* 41, no. 4: 391-403.

Kagan, Jerome. 2006. *An Argument for Mind*. New Haven: Yale University Press.

Kant, Immanuel. 1990 [1781]. *Critique of Pure Reason*, trans. by J. M. D. Meiklejohn. Buffalo, NY: Prometheus Books.

Kim, Kyung-Sun and Allen, Bryce. 2002. "Cognitive and Task Influences on Web Searching Behavior" *Journal of the American Society for Information Science* 53, no. 2: 109-19.

Kuhlthau, Carol C. 2004. *Seeking Meaning: A Process Approach to Library and Information Services*, 2nd ed. Westport, CT: Libraries Unlimited.

Lakoff, George. 1987. *Women, Fire, and Dangerous Things: What Categories Reveal about the Mind*. Chicago: University of Chicago Press.

Lehrer, Jonah. 2009. *How We Decide*. Boston: Houghton Mifflin Harcourt.

Levinas, Emmanuel. 1979. *Totality and Infinity: An Essay on Exteriority*, trans. by Alphonso Lingis. Pittsburgh, Duquesne University Press.

Lindauer, Bonnie Gratch. 2004. "The Three Arenas of Information Literacy Assessment." *Reference & User Services Quarterly* 44, no. 2: 122-29.

Losee, Robert M. 1997. "A Discipline Independent Definition of Information." *Journal of the American Society for Information Science* 48, no. 3: 254-69.

Lycan, William G., ed.. 1990. *Mind and Cognition*. Cambridge, MA: Basil Blackwell.

Macpherson, Karen. 2004. "An Information Processing Model of Undergraduate Electronic Database Information Retrieval." *Journal of the American Society for Information Science* 55, no. 4: 333-47.

McGinn, Colin. 1999. *The Mysterious Flame: Conscious Minds in a Material World*. New York: Basic Books.

Mayer, Richard E., Heiser, Julie, and Lonn, Steve. 2001. "Cognitive Constraints on Multimedia Learning: When Presenting More Material Results in Less Learning. *Journal of Educational Psychology* 93, no. 1: 187-98.

Merleau-Ponty, Maurice. 1962. *Phenomenology of Perception*. Trans. by Colin Smith. London: Routledge.

Moran, Dermot. 2005. *Husserl: Founder of Phenomenology*. Cambridge: Polity.

Naismith, Rachel and Stein, Joan. 1989. "Library Jargon: Student Comprehension of Technical Language Used by Librarians." *College & Research Libraries* 50, no. 4: 543-52.

Neely, Teresa Y. 2006. *Information Literacy Assessment: Standards-Based Tools and Assignments*. Chicago: ALA.

Nietfield, John L., Cao, Li, and Osborne, Jason W. 2005. "Metacognitive Monitoring Accuracy and Student Performance in the Postsecondary Classroom." *The Journal of Experimental Education* 74, no. 1: 7-28.

Orme, William A. 2004. "The Study of the Residual Impact of the Texas Information Literacy Tutorial on the Information-Seeking Ability of First-Year College Students." *College & Research Libraries* 65, no. 3: 205-15.

Owusu-Ansah, Edward K. 2003. "Information Literacy and the Academic Library: A Critical Look at a Concept and the Controversies Surrounding It." *Journal of Academic Librarianship* 29, no. 4: 219-30.

Paas, Fred, Renkl, Alexander, and Sweller, John. 2003. "Cognitive Load Theory and Instructional Design: Recent Developments." *Educational Psychologist* 38, no. 1: 1-4.

Papineau, David. 2003. *The Roots of Reason: Philosophical Essays on Rationality, Evolution, and Probability.* Oxford: Clarendon Press.

Prins, Frans, Veenman, Marcel V. J., and Elshout, Jan J. 2006. "The Impact of Intellectual Ability and Metacognition on Learning: New Support for the Threshold of Problematic Theory." *Learning and Instruction* 16, no. 4: 374-87.

Putnam, Hilary. 2002. *The Collapse of the Fact/Value Dichotomy: And Other Essays.* Cambridge, MA: Harvard University Press.

Rader, Hannelore. 1999. "Faculty-Librarian Collaboration in Building the Curriculum for the Millennium: The US Experience." *IFLA Journal* 25, no. 4: 209-13.

Ricoeur, Paul. 1976. *Interpretation Theory: Discourse and the Surplus of Meaning.* Forth Worth: Texas Christian University Press.

Ricoeur, Paul. 2000. *The Just.* Trans. by David Pellauer. Chicago: University of Chicago Press.

Ricoeur, Paul. 1992. *Oneself as Another.* Trans. by Kathleen Blamey. Chicago: University of Chicago Press.

Ricoeur, Paul. 2005. *The Course of Recognition.* Trans. by David Pellauer. Cambridge, MA: Harvard University Press.

Rockman, Ilene F. 2005. "Information and Communication Technology Literacy: New Assessments for Higher Education." *College and Research Libraries News* 66, no. 8: 587-89.

Rose, Steven P. R. 2005. *The Future of the Brain: The Promise and Perils of Tomorrow's Neuroscience.* Oxford: Oxford University Press.

Russell, Matheson. 2006. *Husserl: A Guide for the Perplexed.* London: Continuum.

Scharf, Davida, Elliot, Norbert, and Huey, Heather A. 2007. "Direct Assessment of Information Literacy Using Writing Portfolios." *Journal of Academic Librarianship* 33, no. 4: 462-77.

Schwartz, Barry. 2004. *The Paradox of Choice: Why More Is Less.* New York: Ecco.

Searle, John R. 2002. *Consciousness and Language*. Cambridge: Cambridge University Press.

Searle, John R. 1997. *The Mystery of Consciousness*. New York: New York Review of Books.

Searle, John R. 2001. *Rationality in Action*. Cambridge, MA: MIT Press.

Shannon, Claude and Weaver, Warren. 1949. *The Mathematical Theory of Communication*. Urbana: University of Illinois Press.

Sharma, Shikha. 2007. "From Chaos to Clarity: Using the Research Portfolio to Teach and Assess Information Literacy Skills." *Journal of Academic Librarianship* 33, no. 1: 127-35.

Simon, Herbert. 1983. *Reason in Human Affairs*. Stanford: Stanford University Press.

Skinner, B. F. 1953. *Science and Human Behavior*. New York: Free Press.

Smith, Laurence D. 1986. *Behaviorism and Logical Positivism: A Reassessment of the Alliance*. Stanford: Stanford University Press.

Sokolowski, Robert. 2000. *Introduction to Phenomenology*. Cambridge: Cambridge University Press.

Spada, Marcantonio, Nikcevic, Ana, Moneta, Giovanni, and Ireson, Judy. 2006. Metacognition as a Mediator of Test Anxiety on a Surface Approach to Studying." *Educational Psychology* 26, no. 5: 615-24.

Stevens, Edward, Jr.. 1987. "The Anatomy of Mass Literacy in Nineteenth-Century United States. In R. F. Arnove and H. J. Graff, eds., *National Literacy Campaigns: Historical and Comparative Perspectives*, pp. 99-122. New York: Plenum.

Taleb, Nassem Nicholas. 2007. *The Black Swan: The Impact of the Highly Improbable*. New York: Random House.

"A Test of Leadership: Charting the Future of U.S. Higher Education." 2006. Washington, DC: U.S. Department of Education.

Tuman, Myron. 2002. *CriticalThinking.com: A Guide to Deep Thinking in a Shallow Age*. Philadelphia: Xlibris Corporation.

Weaver, Warren. 1949. "The Mathematics of Communication." *Scientific American* 181, no. 1: 11-15.

Webber, Sheila Anne Elizabeth and Johnston, Bill. 2000. "Conceptions of Information Literacy." *Journal of Information Science* 26, no. 6: 381-97.

Webster, Frank. 1995. *Theories of the Information Society*. London: Routledge.

Wells, Gordon. 1999. *Dialogic Inquiry: Towards a Sociocultural Practice and Theory of Education*. Cambridge: Cambridge University Press.

Wilder Stanley. 2005. "Information Literacy Makes All the Wrong Assumptions." *Chronicle of Higher* Education 51, no. 18: B13.

Williams, Peter. 2006. "Against Information Literacy." *Library and Information Update* 5, nos. 7/8: 20.

Willis, Carolyn N. and Thomas, Wm. Joseph. 2006. "Students as Audience: Identity and Information Literacy Instruction." *portal: Libraries and the Academy* 6, no. 4: 431-44.

Wittgenstein, Ludwig. 1974. *Philosophical Grammar*. Trans. by A. Kenny. Berkeley: University of California Press.

Zabel, Diane. 2004. "A Reaction to 'Information Literacy and Higher Education.'" *Journal of Academic Librarianship* 30, no. 1: 17-21.

Zahavi, Dan. 2003. *Husserl's Phenomenology*. Stanford: Stanford University Press.

Zipf, George K. 1949. *Human Behavior and the Principle of Least Effort*. Cambridge, MA: Addison-Wesley.

Index